HAUNTED
MUSKEGON

HAUNTED
MUSKEGON

MARIE HELENA CISNEROS

Published by Haunted America
A division of The History Press
Charleston, SC
www.historypress.com

Unless otherwise noted, all photographs are courtesy of the author.

First published 2022

Manufactured in the United States

ISBN 9781467150217

Library of Congress Control Number: 2022936207

Notice: The information in this book is true and complete to the best of our knowledge. It is offered without guarantee on the part of the author or The History Press. The author and The History Press disclaim all liability in connection with the use of this book.

CONTENTS

ACKNOWLEDGEMENTS

Writing this book is the culmination of a lifelong dream to be a writer. But dreams are the easy part. Doing the work to the best of one's ability and dedicating oneself to its completion is a lot harder. It is also richly rewarding. Nevertheless, I couldn't have done it alone, and I am eternally grateful for the help and encouragement of so many who helped make this happen. First of all, I'd like to thank family and friends who encouraged me, embraced my "weirdness" and understood my lifelong obsession to understand as much I could about all things mysterious, hidden or strange. To Andy O'Riley of O'Riley Media Group, PositivelyMuskegon.com and MuskegonChannel.com, I owe a deep debt of gratitude. His love, community service and dedication to building a brighter future for Muskegon are unsurpassed. My dream may never have come to pass if he had not taken a chance on me, someone totally inexperienced at being in front of a camera but who had an idea for a "paranormal show." Andy turned me into a reporter and a media host. My sincere gratitude and appreciation goes out to Gabe Schillman of Studio 37 Arts, who has graciously provided his extraordinary artistic talents to this work, adding depth and complexity to my stories. His bold and skillfully rendered black-and-white illustrations and inspired representation of the Hume House make pivotal statements, bringing modern realism to the buildings. They attract the eye and serve as captivating focal points along the story lines.

I want to thank the paranormal researchers and ghost hunters for sharing their knowledge, expertise and stories with me for this work. I am grateful for the opportunity to give readers an in-depth look at their investigative methods as well as a few of their investigations. Their diligence and emphasis on investigating using scientific methods as well as intuition add a much-needed level of validity and professionalism to the field of the paranormal. It is important work. Hopefully, *Haunted Muskegon* will serve to help educate and enrich their understanding of paranormal research, as well as entertain. My sincere appreciation goes to the following: Dan Schmidt of Kent County Paranormal and Brandon Hoezee of Grand Rapids Ghost Hunters for their help with Torrent House and the LST 393; Darren Dykhouse of Lakeshore Paranormal for help with LST 393 and Nunica Cemetery; Candi and Rick Hess of Great Lakes Spirit Seekers for their help with the pastry shop ghosts and Nunica Cemetery; Connie and Bill Jones of GRASPP for their help with the LST 393 ghosts; Deanna Hadley of West Michigan Paranormal Team for her help with the pastry shop ghosts; and Shetan Noir of *Squatch GQ* magazine for her help with the Christmas tree ship disappearance. Last but certainly not least, many thanks to Mallory Metzger and the entire staff at Hackley Library's Torrent House Local History and Genealogy Department. Their kindness and support with my research and documentation were invaluable and made creating my project so much easier. For anyone doing research, for whatever reason, there is infinitely more to it than putting words into a search bar. For this reason, the services that librarians provide to researchers are vital. Libraries are the gateways to knowledge, and librarians are the key to these gateways, opening doors to future generations. Thank you one and all. You are all appreciated.

INTRODUCTION

Most people enjoy a good ghost story, even if they don't believe in ghosts. Others like them more if they think they might be real. To that end, I hope this book will both entertain and inform. If you're someone who is fascinated by things that make the hair on the back of your neck stand up or send a cold shiver down your spine, then Muskegon, Michigan, may be just the place for you. What might not be known to the tourists who flock to the area in the summer months is that Muskegon has a few ghosts in residence—according to local stories, anyway. There are even whispers among some locals that all of Muskegon is haunted. This, of course, is probably an exaggeration, but there have been some pretty strange goings-on. In fact, the ghost stories, instead of fading away, have continued, because it appears the ghosts are still being seen around town. The fact that these stories haven't faded into oblivion like a spectral shadow should be taken into consideration. Perhaps a serious study is in order. From the ethereal wanderings of an elegant showman in a luxurious 1940s-era theater, a ghostly pastry shop customer and the apparition of the city's founding father in a library, to shadowy deckhands on a World War II warship museum, it appears that Muskegon, Michigan, is indeed haunted. Who or what these ghosts are is a matter of opinion. Because when it comes to ghosts, any cut-and-dried evidence to their reality is pretty much unverifiable. Thus, the divide between the skeptics and believers continues to be wide, no matter what the evidence. While modern devices and instrumentation have lent credibility and integrity to ghost research, a lot of information is based on anecdotal evidence and eyewitness testimony, which can be unreliable or faulty. Thus, unfortunately, there has been no "smoking gun" to prove the existence of ghosts to a definitive extent. As a consequence, these stories may continue to be seen in the same light as urban legends or folklore: entertaining and thrilling, but fiction nonetheless. On a positive note, scientific theories on the source of hauntings, ghosts and apparitions have given possible affirmation to their reality—if objective reality can be assumed. These theories are varied and cover a range of scientific disciplines, from meteorology to psychology or physics. Ghost hunters and paranormal investigators are striving to find answers to the question of ghosts. A few of Muskegon's rumored haunted buildings have been investigated, including several of the homes discussed here.

It is imaginable that they are just faint glimmers of Muskegon's gilded age caught in time, a time of extravagance, romance and glamour of bygone days that still lingers to cast shadows on the landscape. They may simply be mists imprinted on the landscape when Native Americans still lived along Muskegon's marshy shores, burying their dead with tools or items for their journey into the afterlife. Perhaps it is the spirits of hardy trappers or lumberjacks who endured hardships and grueling work amid the wilderness and bitter Michigan winters that still wander the land as shadows. Under such harsh conditions, and in such uncertain times, it was not uncommon to meet with an early or untimely death. Any or all of these phantoms may yet roam restlessly over the land Muskegon was built upon, or in the buildings or houses that remain. If so, perhaps they only do so to be acknowledged, even if they can't be counted on any city census.

IF YOU WERE TO walk along the city streets of Muskegon, Michigan, on any given day, you would find it quite lively and charming. Most people who live here are well acquainted with what Muskegon has to offer and are proud of their city. From Ottawan Native village to booming lumbering town to industrial hub, Muskegon has blossomed into a thriving and vibrant tourist town. However, it has been a long, arduous road from that small Ottawan village to thriving tourist hub, with a lot of twists and turns and ups and downs, but it is all the stronger for it. All in all, Muskegonites love their town, and first-time visitors to the area usually want to return again and again, sometimes making it their home. With its beaches, events and varied shopping scene with a unique feel, the city has become a "boomtown"

Muskegon Chronicle building.

Café Muskegon sign. Former Wierengo Hotel building.

once again. However, it has taken much determination, inspiration and sustained efforts to turn a factory town into a tourist city. There are now over 175,000 people living in and around the city. Growth within the city has been relatively stable, with a population of 36,565 in 2019. There was only minimal loss since the 2010 census. It's true that Muskegon has seen a lot of changes in the past. No doubt it will change in the future. All cities do. However, one thing is for certain: Muskegon's lumber-town spirit remains strong. If Muskegon gets knocked down, it will be sure to get right back up.

Muskegon's downtown progressed over the years, from store-lined streets in the 1930s and '40s to a mall in the '70s, and it now embraces a diverse and eclectic array of shopping and entertainment experiences. Aspiring to honor Muskegon's rich industrial past and make use of the structures that remained, many family-owned businesses have cropped up in refurbished factories, closed stores and clubhouses. With the growing national trend of craft beers, Muskegon has seen an influx of microbreweries and pub-style establishments cropping up, reinvigorating and building on the town's long history of beer making. This began with the establishment of the Muskegon

Fire truck and dog sign. Former Wierengo Hotel building.

USS Silversides Museum.

Brewery Company in 1877. Muskegon Brewery's claim to fame was being one of only two breweries in the world that bottled Guinness beer. With the shops, pubs and restaurants establishing themselves in these vintage and iconic buildings, the downtown area now has a warm and inviting look, harkening back to Muskegon's Romantic era. Victorian-style lampposts dot the streets, casting a warm glow on the evening. Many businesses display artifacts and decor from past eras. Muskegon has become a premier spot along the lake to enjoy the company of friends, good food, beverages, events and music. This is especially true when summer comes to Michigan.

Muskegon has an amazing assortment of fun things to do in the summer, including music events, theater productions, art galleries and pop-up craft shows, as well as unique shops to browse to your heart's content. For those looking to add some learning to their summer outings, there are numerous museums, including the USS Silversides Museum, the LST 393 Veterans Museum and the Lakeshore Museum Center. Lakeshore Museum Center comprises numerous buildings, including a history museum, archives, the Fire Barn Museum, the Depression-era Scolnik House and the Hackley and Hume Historic Site. For foodies,

Above: Mastodon statue. Lakeshore Museum Center. *Sculpture by Gille and Marc, 2019.*

Left: Pier at Pere Marquette Beach.

Opposite: Sailboat on Lake Michigan.

Muskegon has a vast range of cuisine to sample, from brick-oven pizza to Thai curry. If you like boating, swimming or just sitting on the beach soaking up the sun, Pere Marquette Park, with its two miles of beach area, has become a popular draw for people from around the country. Nothing says summer like a refreshing swim at the beach followed by a stop at a local ice cream shop. In summer months, the park is also the site of volleyball tournaments, parasailing, kite flying and family outings. If you prefer taking a leisurely stroll or biking, Lakeshore Trail along Muskegon Lake has a twenty-five-mile path suitable for walking, hiking and biking.

Situated along the banks of Muskegon Lake, an inlet of Lake Michigan, Muskegon started out as Masquigon, an Ottawa Indian village, around 1839. The name roughly translates to "marshy swamp" in the Ottawa language. Human habitation in Michigan goes back to at least ten thousand to fourteen thousand years ago after the last Ice Age. The Paleo-Indians are traditionally said to have come down through the Bering Strait by way of Alaska. Later on, tribes such as the Ottawa, Chippewa and Pottawatomi, part of the Algonquin family of Native Americans, began making seasonal settlements along its shores. These tribes migrated from place to place, following the seasons, animal migrations and buffalo herds. The Ottawa traded among neighboring tribes in cornmeal, sunflower oil, furs and tobacco, as well as medicinal plants. The Ottawa, migrating from Canada, Ohio and the East Coast first arrived in Michigan's Upper Peninsula before spreading out over the lower region. After the signing of the Treaty of Detroit, the United States was given large swaths of southeastern Michigan and sections of Ohio.

Michigan, as a territory, was at various times under both French and British control. The first outpost was located at Saint Ignace in 1668. Michigan became a state in 1837, with Muskegon County being established in 1859. The early history of the Muskegon area is somewhat murky, but it is believed that the French had been familiar with the area since the seventeenth century. Muskegon is known to have been listed on maps as early as the 1700s. For over one hundred years, life in Michigan centered on the fur trade, with French pioneers establishing trading posts, missions and forts. The fur trade was a major feature in early exploration of the Great Lakes before the area was settled by Europeans, thus trappers and the early indigenous tribes composed much of the area's inhabitants. French explorers had reached the Michigan coastline early on, setting up fur-trading posts in and around Muskegon Lake and beginning trade with Native Americans. Unfortunately, the French greatly exploited the fur trade in the colonial era, impacting the lives of these early inhabitants, who were greatly sought after as scouts and trading partners. These Native American scouts would paddle up and down the waterways of the Great Lakes in birch bark canoes loaded with pelts, goods and supplies. In exchange for furs, they would receive European goods such as iron tools, cloth and beads. The Native Americans were also supplied with firearms and liquor in exchanges, both of which had a detrimental impact on their lives and culture. Locations of French trading posts in Muskegon are not well known, but we do have record of a few trappers. It is known that explorer Father (Pere) Jacques Marquette passed through the area with a party of French soldiers in 1679 under the command of Henry DeTonty. Marquette was a French Jesuit missionary who founded Michigan's first European settlement at Sault Ste. Marie, in the Upper Peninsula. One of the earliest known fur trappers in the Muskegon area was a man named Edward Fitzgerald. He is said to have lived in the area in 1748 and died in White Lake. Another French Canadian trapper, Joseph LaFramboise, established a trading post near the mouth of Duck Lake. Other early settlers included Lamar Andie, Jean Baptiste Recollect and Pierre Constant. Little is known of these early Muskegon dwellers. When fur trading and trapping waned, settlers began arriving, bringing with them the need for food, supplies, tools, transportation and housing. The meteoric rise of Muskegon's lumber industry, with the ensuing building of sawmills, railroads and ships, saw many of those needs met.

Muskegon grew to become a bustling hub of commerce. Trains brought in travelers as well as goods. Ships, many built or financed by Muskego's wealthy lumber barons, transported goods from around the country and the world, as well as exported lumber. With the addition of the Michigan Territory, and after the forests of Maine and New York State had yielded all they could, Michigan began to be eyed as an important new source for lumber. Muskegon soon became the epicenter for that industry. Beginning in 1837, Muskegon became a key competitor in the lumber industry with forty-seven sawmills dotting the banks of the Muskegon River. Northern Michigan forests were lush with pines—Norway, jack and white. Forests in the lower half of Michigan were teeming with hardwoods, coveted for their beauty and durability. But it was the massive white pine, some over two hundred feet in height and over five feet in diameter, that drove the industry in Michigan. The promise of steady work and the possibility of striking it rich brought the lumberjacks to Muskegon in droves. Many of them were farm boys looking to make extra money during the winter months.

Muskegon, producing more lumber than any other city in the world, became a boomtown bustling with vitality, opportunity and ambition. The world cried out for lumber, and Muskegon was more than ready and willing to supply it. Numerous sawmills cropped up along the lakes, running at full speed day and night. There was the constant din of enterprising resourcefulness and fortitude. This desire and need for more lumber drove the industry at a breakneck pace, with over 660 million board feet cut in one year alone. Unfortunately, this boom was not to last. By 1890, most of the trees had been cut down and hundreds of acres of land cleared, leaving wastelands. The lumberjacks were able to eke out a modest living from the enterprise, but work was grueling and conditions harsh. Logs were typically cut in the winter, transported by horse-drawn sleds to be stacked along the riverbanks until spring before being floated downriver to the sawmills. Easier and swifter methods of production were sought. Railroads provided an answer. Following the invention of steam-powered engines in 1807, railways were becoming the premier mode of transport. The first railroad track was laid in 1830, running only thirteen miles. Ten years later, the Northeast and Middle Atlantic states were connected by track, and by 1860, much of the eastern region was joined. Logging was a major factor in the building of these railroad lines, as larger lumber companies needed a way to ship the product as well

Pere Marquette train caboose.

as bring in workers, horses, food and supplies. In an effort to transport the large volume of lumber going out from Muskegon mills, as well as goods and passengers, railroads connecting Muskegon to Chicago were soon constructed. With the building of railway systems, the laborious sleds used by lumbermen to transport logs soon became a thing of the past.

The Chicago and Michigan Lake Shore Railroad ran from around 1870 until 1881; connections to New Buffalo, Holland and Pentwater were eventually built. The C&MLS later added two other lines from Holland to Grand Rapids. Eventually, this railroad changed hands, reorganized as the Chicago and West Michigan Railroad. Another branch went to Grand Haven. In 1881, the Grand Rapids and Indiana Railroad and the Muskegon, Saginaw and Toledo Railway were constructed, with two more lines being run to Muskegon. After the existing depot was found to be in extremely poor condition, the Union Depot was built to accommodate increasing railway use and traffic coming and going into Muskegon. The depot was eventually taken over by the Pere Marquette Railroad, which operated in the Great Lakes region as well as parts of Ontario. The Pere Marquette had connections in Michigan, Ohio, Indiana and Ontario, with primary connections to Buffalo, Toledo and Chicago. The Pere Marquette

Wagon at Union Depot.

was later absorbed by the Chesapeake and Ohio (C&O) system. By the 1930s, the Muskegon, Saginaw and Toledo Railway had been acquired by the Grand Trunk system and began using a different station than Union Depot. In 1938, another change in systems resulted in the system being taken over by the Pennsylvania Railroad, which began using the same station as Grand Trunk. Union Depot continued to operate as a destination of the Midnight Express from Chicago, but with the rise of automobile use, and with the decline in the lumber industry, use of trains dwindled significantly. In the wake of the demise of the lumber industry, the depot was used as the main railroad terminal, accommodating passengers. In 1971, passenger operation ceased, although freight service continued for several more years. The depot ceased all operations in 1978, and the building stood empty until the 1990s. Union Depot had the distinction of bringing numerous prominent visitors to Muskegon, including William Jennings Bryan, Richard M. Nixon and Harry S Truman. The building was donated to the county in 1992 and currently serves as the Muskegon Convention and Visitors Bureau. A small railway museum in the building houses artifacts, photos and memorabilia of Muskegon's railroad history.

Union Depot dedication plaque. 1895.

Union Depot building. Muskegon County Convention and Visitors Bureau.

The belief at the time that Michigan's forests would supply lumber for hundreds of years was a rather grim fairy tale. It only took twenty years to decimate Michigan's forests. Because it was so highly prized in construction, the white pine was especially hard hit. Unfortunately, other species were depleted as well; many species of pines, conifers and hardwoods fell to the axe. In looking at the lumber industry from a twenty-first-century perspective, we take a dim view that vast expanses of virgin forests were cleared so completely of trees, many never re-growing. From a nineteenth-century perspective, construction and creating farmland were top priorities. Farmland was felt to be of greater value than forests, which were considered wastelands or a resource to be used. Replanting didn't seem to be of concern. If it did occur, it was an expensive endeavor and a long-term undertaking. It takes more than seventy years to regrow forestland. One positive result from the expansion of the lumber industry was its value in the building and growing of America. A large percentage of the timber used in construction in the United States came from Michigan forests. Agnes Larson, writing on the harvesting of the white pine in Minnesota, believed that it resulted in the region being settled rapidly along with people better able to afford building homes, which helped to increase economic growth nationally. By the end of the lumber boom, almost twenty million acres of Michigan forests had been stripped clean, some never to recover. These wastelands were referred to as "stump prairies." Some of the land was resold as farmland, some reverted to the state. The lumber company of Charles Hackley and Thomas Hume owned over three hundred thousand acres of timberland in Arkansas, Louisiana, Mississippi and South Carolina in addition to their holdings in Muskegon.

Some have likened the lumber era to the gold rush of California. It certainly seemed that way. There was plenty of money to be made. Cities around the country were booming, and businesses were flourishing. The biographies of several of Muskegon's lumber barons read like Charles Dickens rags-to-riches novels, in which a poor but industrious hero overcomes insurmountable odds to become rich and famous. Many of these founders of Muskegon did have humble beginnings. They were young and ambitious but had little cash. Still, they were able to rise to great wealth and prominence. Whether or not they were heroes is a matter of opinion; nevertheless, more than a few millionaires were made at this time. Men like Charles Hackley, Thomas Hume, A.V. Mann, John Torrent and others became known as "lumber barons" and were instrumental in ushering in what is known in these parts as the Romantic era of Muskegon.

These wealthy and enterprising industrialists pumped a lot of money into the economy and the growing community. A few of them lived lavishly for the times and the area, building grand mansions for themselves and their families. Wanting only the best, they used the finest imported goods and materials. Some of these mansions were built using lumber extracted from Michigan's own forests. America was enthralled with the idea of new technologies and new ways of obtaining products. Factory-made and ready-made products were becoming more commonplace and desirable. More people were able to afford such luxuries, and those with disposable incomes also wanted this elegance and grace for their homes. To accommodate their elegant tastes and needs, plenty of designers and architects were more than willing to fulfill their extravagant whims, often creating unique and sometimes even excessive houses. One such opulent mansion was built by A.V. Mann. The son of a lawyer from New Jersey, Mann came to the Muskegon area when it was still a frontier town of only six hundred inhabitants. Taking advantage of the lumbering boom early on, he bought land on Cedar Creek and eventually became one of Muskegon's wealthiest and most powerful men. No small feat in a town said to have more millionaires living here than in the whole country. Mann's colossal twenty-eight-room mansion was constructed of imported brick, with nine-foot ceilings and cornices of hand-carved wood. There were seven fireplaces, imported French glass and breathtakingly beautiful staircases. Costing $20,000 to build in the 1800s, at today's prices this mansion would be worth $425,000. The houses belonging to John Torrent, Charles Hackley and Thomas Hume also stand as powerful testaments to their success as businessmen, entrepreneurs and philanthropists. Their mansions are also an outward statement of their love of luxury and splendor. While most of these grand houses and buildings from the lumber barons' heyday have crumbled to dust, some are still standing 184 years later. Some of these may very well be haunted.

Charles Hackley came to Muskegon in 1856, and Thomas Hume arrived in 1870. They became partners in 1881, opening up lumber mills and sawmills, building ships and bringing in railroads. While many of the lumber barons chose to leave the city after the mills closed, Hackley and Hume decided to remain in the area, becoming chief proponents, along with other industrialists, of revitalizing the city. Through their efforts, they encouraged businesses to relocate to Muskegon, thus providing jobs to stem the flow of labor leaving for greener pastures. Some of Charles Hackley's gifts to the city include Hackley Public Library, Hackley Art Gallery, Hackley Park, Hackley School, Hackley Stadium, Hackley Hospital and the City of Muskegon

St. Paul's Episcopal Church.

Poor Fund Endowment. At the time, these endowments were valued at over $12 million—in today's market, probably $1 billion or more. As these establishments continue to enrich the lives of those living today, they can be considered priceless. Muskegon's unique and vibrant lumbering history is honored and celebrated today. There is a keen interest in preserving that history with informational lectures, interactive and informative exhibits and even entertaining historical events such as the Lumber Baron's Ball. This elegant and popular event has been a Muskegon staple for many years. The highlight of the evening is a visit from none other than Charles Hackley himself—rather, someone dressed as him, not his ghost.

Muskegon has always been a good place to live, work and raise children, although it has not been without adversity, disasters and, occasionally, a bit of mayhem. In October 1919, four people died and fourteen went missing when a passenger steamship coming from Milwaukee broke apart as it made its way through the darkened harbor. Most of the passengers were asleep when the incident took place, some barely getting away in their nightclothes. Within minutes, the ship had sunk beneath the water. In another tragic incident, two interurban trolley drivers were killed when a

Left: Statue of Lincoln in Hackley Park. *Sculpture by Charles H. Nichaus, 1898.*

Right: Statue of Ulysses S. Grant in Hackley Park. *Sculpture by J. Massey Rhind, 1898.*

freight car from Grand Rapids collided with a passenger car from Muskegon on a curve. While a rarity, even murder was not unheard of. In June 1899, J.W. Taylor, said to have been livid that his efforts to seek office were thwarted, turned his rage on Muskegon's mayor, James Balbirnie, gunning him down in cold blood as he stood in the door of his business. Taylor then committed suicide by drinking carbolic acid and shooting himself, dying within minutes.

But one of the most lurid and controversial stories to have come out of Muskegon is that of Nathan Douglas. In April 1895, Douglas died under suspicious circumstances. His daughter Eunice Williams suspected the druggist, George W. King, of poisoning him. King was arrested, along with his aunt, a Mary Houston or Hughson, who had recently married Douglas. Soon after the couple wed, the druggist was seen visiting Douglas. Within days of King's visit, Douglas was dead. When Williams went to the police with her suspicions, the body was exhumed and found to contain a large amount of poison. It was later discovered that Mary's first husband had also died under suspicious circumstances five years earlier. Rumors soon became circulating in Muskegon that this Mary Hughson (or Houston) was none other than the notorious Kate Bender, a member of the "Bloody Benders" of Kansas. The Bender family was said to have murdered upward of a dozen people in rural Kansas around the same time. While it was only rumor that Mary Hughson and Kate Bender were the same person, it is believed by some that the Benders had been living in the Muskegon area under assumed names before relocating to Kansas. Muskegon County sheriff William H. Smith was the arresting officer of Mary Douglas and George King. Kate Bender disappeared from the Kansas area, and according to Smith, evidence pointed to Mary Hughson being Kate. When questioned about the Douglas murder, Mary was said to have displayed an inordinate amount of interest in the Benders, raising suspicions. After no charges were filed against her in Douglas's death, she disappeared from Muskegon. She later turned up in Battle Creek, where, coincidently, the Benders were confined. Sheriff Smith had seen Mary Hughson, aka Kate Bender, many times during the Douglas investigation and felt there was strong evidence to confirm that Mary was indeed Kate Bender. If Kate and her family did spend time in the Muskegon area, it is possible, given their propensity to do away with people that they did away with a few others. With the murders of Mayor Balbirnie, Nathan Douglas and George King and the suicide of J.W. Taylor looming over Muskegon's past, as well as the tendency of spirits to haunt the scenes of their deaths, they may well be still among Muskegon's spectral citizens.

Consequently, with all the ghostly rumors circulating in the Muskegon area, it should come as no surprise to find out that there are a number of adventurous and inquisitive paranormal investigative teams willing to discover what tales the dead have to tell. In fact, at least four Michigan investigative teams have done extensive studies into these rumors and reports of paranormal activity in the area. Several of the buildings and sites will be discussed here. The teams use a variety of electronic devices as well as their own abilities to communicate with spirits. Some intriguing data has been produced, which many feel lends credibility to the idea that something very unusual and paranormal is happening.

INVESTIGATORS, METHODS AND EQUIPMENT

When a building or home is beset by unexplained phenomena or thought to be haunted, some key questions arise that need to be answered: What was seen? What caused it? Can a rational explanation be found? If no rational explanation can be found, then calling in a paranormal investigator might be a good idea, especially if you suspect something paranormal is going on. Even so, conclusive evidence that the spirit survives death or that the spiritual body can get trapped on the earthy plane is still a point of contention between believers and skeptics. That divide will probably continue for the foreseeable future. But believing in ghosts is no modern idea. People have long believed that spirits, ghosts or apparitions walk the earth and can even interact with us from time to time. In fact, this belief has been with us since the dawn of time in cultures around the world. It continues today. A 2015 Pew Research survey found that over one-third of Americans believe in life after death. A 2013 Harris poll found that over 42 percent of Americans believe in the existence of ghosts, with one in five Americans stating that they have either seen or been in the presence of a ghost and 29 percent reported being in touch with someone in the spirit world. There is also a belief that spirits have the ability to interact with us or affect us in the living realm. Some believe that the world of the spirits is all around us and affects us in many ways. These energies are subtle and go unnoticed for the most part. These can range from a typical ghost sighting to a more frightening interaction, with negative energies or entities that can manifest physical effects or exert a variety of ailments on those unlucky enough to encounter them. However, believing in something isn't proof of that thing's existence, and eyewitness accounts, while important, can be passed off as imagination, misidentification or outright hoax. For this reason, evidence gathered by qualified, independent researchers can help support the case for the reality of these otherworldly manifestations. Some researchers, on the other hand, believe that apparitions, demons and even extraterrestrial encounters can be attributed to the witness being in a hypnogogic state. This is a type of hallucination that results from one being halfway between awake and asleep. These states used to be called "night terrors." Sometimes, they are accompanied by sleep paralysis, as the person's body is still in a sleeping state, while the conscious mind is awake. Even so, it is still up to the individual to weigh the evidence and make up their own minds as to the reality of ghosts. At any rate, their existence, or lack thereof, is a relevant and intriguing subject to ponder, if only for the love of reading a spine-chilling story on a cold, blustery night.

There are upward of two hundred paranormal groups working in Michigan, including fifteen operating in the West Michigan area and several in Muskegon. Each group has its own focus, organizational setup and methods. They range from loosely organized groups of like-minded individuals who get together as friends, to full-fledged, incorporated companies or nonprofit organizations. Even so, they all generally strive to seek answers to unusual or mysterious events, bring attention to the phenomenon and educate the public. For the most part, the goal is to use investigative methods, equipment and a scientific approach to either disprove or prove an event as something "paranormal." A key element is for an investigator to go into each investigation with an open mind and a skeptical intellect. Many of these individuals have entered into the field as a result of unexplained events that either they or their families have experienced, as well as curiosity about the unknown and mysterious side of life and what happens when we die. Paranormal investigators come from a broad assortment of fields and careers, from former military personnel and executives to housewives and retirees. Often, these groups will collaborate in group investigations, as has been done in the Muskegon area on several investigations. Paranormal investigators use a variety of methods in their quest to find spirits, including electronic devices, psychic mediums and channeling their own empathic and intuitive gifts. Darren Dykhouse has always had a fascination for the mysterious and has had lifelong paranormal experiences. He began investigating the paranormal in 2013, first by using voice recorder apps on his phone. He founded Lakeshore Paranormal in 2018 and has investigated a number of sites in the Muskegon area, including the LST 393 Veterans Museum, as well as Nunica and Oakwood Cemeteries. His investigative videos on the Lakeshore Paranormal media channel have brought attention to many rumored hauntings throughout the state. Darren considers himself to be an "empath" with a special gift for sensing when spirits are present. He uses this ability in his investigations, as well as a variety of electronic and digital devices and cellphone applications, including instrumental transcommunication devices, a spirit box SB7-T (a device that phases out white noise), a necrophonic phone app and digital recorders. Darren has worked with other area paranormal investigators, including Bill and Connie Jones of GRASPP, Brandon Hoezee and the Kent County Paranormal Team.

West Michigan Paranormal Team was founded in 2018 by Candi Hess and Deanna Hadley of Muskegon. The team used an assortment of instruments in their work, including voice recorders, SLS cameras, K2 meters, spirit boxes, dowsing rods, EMF trigger objects, motion detectors and, occasionally, cat toys. Deanna and Candi also relied on their keen intuitive and empathic skills. The West Michigan Paranormal Team was instrumental in investigating the Frauenthal Theater as well as other buildings.

Kent County Paranormal is a nonprofit investigative organization based in Grand Rapids, Michigan. They strive to assist people in dealing with paranormal activity and are devoted to helping families with paranormal problems. The team uses cameras, thermal cameras and voice recorders. The team began in 2012 as Grand Rapids Ghost Hunters, changing its name to Kent County Paranormal around 2019. It has investigated suspected hauntings in locations all over western Michigan, including Torrent House and the LST 393 ship museum. In addition to using electronic devices in their work, they also use their intuitional skills. Daniel Schmidt is a scryer, and Brandon Hoezee is an empath.

Gathering Research and Stories of Paranormal Phenomena (GRASPP), founded by Bill and Connie Jones, is a paranormal LLC located in Grand Haven, Michigan. Their stated mission is to find answers "about the things that go bump in the night" as well as to educate others about the paranormal. They research and investigate the paranormal throughout the West Michigan and Upper Peninsula areas. GRASPP has been actively ghost hunting for over fifteen years, starting out their adventures one Halloween night with a spur-of-the-moment ghost hunt at Nunica Cemetery. The team has about ten full-time members. Bill reported that they have learned a lot about the subject over the years and enjoy sharing the evidence they have gained, as well as educating those with questions about the paranormal. "We truly believe that knowledge is the key to the answers we seek, and we need everyone to help gather that knowledge." The team uses scientific equipment, methods and techniques that have been used by generations of paranormal investigators. They also use electronic voice phenomena equipment, the Estes Session system and recording programs in order to capture disembodied voices and communications from the spiritual realm. The Estes system uses sensory deprivation in an attempt to capture evidence. These sessions may take several hours to perform. It can take anywhere from two hundred to four hundred hours to analyze data collected from an investigation. GRASPP also employs a wide range of other electronic devices, such as motion sensors, Mel-Meters, EMF detectors, video and audio recorders, IR lights and, occasionally, dowsing rods. Like the members of many other paranormal groups, they also rely on their keen powers of observation and employ those with empathic and intuitive skills to pick up on the energies generated by the spirit realm.

One type of evidence that investigators strive to detect are electromagnetic frequencies, which they believe indicate the presence of ghosts. They do this with the use of specialized cameras and K2 meters. Many also use a device called a "spirit box," which scans radio frequencies to detect electronic voice phenomena. An SB7 spirit box forces radio signals into bits of randomized noise, which the spirits can apparently manipulate into audible sound to communicate. In this way, a spirit box can pick up discarnate voices and other information from the spirit realm. Heat-sensing devices are often used to look for drastic changes in temperature and coldness. While these temperature fluctuations may have natural explanations, historically, they have been accepted as indicating the presence of spirits. Orbs and unusual mists are also considered to be indicators of the presence of spirits and other paranormal activity. Factors such as photographic artifacts or light reflections are routinely examined in such investigations. Another popular ghost-hunting tool is an electromagnetic field (EMF) device. These meters were designed to identify changes in electromagnetic energy fields. Such fluctuations are believed to be evidence of spiritual communication.

One new tool, the SLS camera, while not made specifically for ghost hunting, soon evolved into one of the field's most intriguing gadgets. A feature of Xbox that allowed players to use motion control to interact more efficiently in select games, Microsoft's Kinect hardware became an accidental boon to ghost hunters. This feature, designed to "see" and track a human body in order to navigate and spot opponents in games, was found to also be picking up other figures in the room or in the house—even when no one was present. Incredibly, some gamers found that some "ghosts" were somehow able to also control the consoles. Ghosts are said to be mischievous. They like manipulating cat toys and playing pranks, so it stands to reason they would like gaming, too. While some gamers thought these effects were glitches in the software, paranormal investigators began to see this as a way of proving the reality of the spirit world. It wasn't long before an enterprising paranormal investigator and inventor by the name of Bill Chappel found a way to use this feature in ghost hunting. With modifications to enable the cameras to run on battery packs, and by being connected to tablets or laptops, they have become a staple in the field of paranormal investigation. They are becoming popular in the field the world over, but whether they are really picking up the presence of ghosts is a matter of conjecture. There is no definitive proof that the cameras are detecting ghosts; perhaps they are picking up images similar to radar mirages. The technology is not foolproof even as a feature of gaming, and misidentification or other false readings are possible even under the best conditions. The cameras are designed to search for anything resembling a person but can fail to detect figures that are present. When working correctly, they will show these figures as points of light connected by lines, resembling stickmen on the monitor. Any change in the angle of the camera can make the figures change position or appear otherwise erratic. The images can also appear to be floating in the air or can completely disappear. Another problem is that the scale is often not compatible with the surroundings; sometimes, the stick figures appear quite small. Moving around with the cameras often gives false positives. The grid, made up of dots and lines, moves, distorting what the camera is picking up.

An instrumental transcommunication device is similar to a spirit box. This device can detect sounds that the human ear cannot hear. As it can also detect electronic voice phenomena, or EVPs, within an area or building, it has become another useful ghost-hunting tool. EVPs are believed to be how spirits communicate with us. It is theorized that spirits or otherworldly entities communicate by the modulation of sound waves that can be recorded, known as transform electronic voice phenomena. In addition, spirits can also communicate in real time—opportunistic EVPs—by changing sounds to form speech through mechanical means. In order for spirits to manifest into the physical realm, move objects or communicate, they need some sort of energy to manipulate and use. It is believed that they use the internal sound of the digital devices, which is then picked up on tape or digital file. One of the newer methods used in ghost hunting is known as the Estes method. Estes is believed to be a sort of channeling conduit for the spirit. This was developed by investigators Karl Pfeiffer, Connor Randall and Michelle Tate in 2016. This method is named for the Colorado city where they lived. The method's popularity in the field of paranormal investigation has grown rapidly since then. Estes works by isolating the white noise from an SB7 spirit box. To begin, an investigator is blindfolded and connected to a spirit box or white-noise generator with headsets in place. With all audio and visual stimuli removed, they sit quietly and are to say whatever comes to them or report what sounds they hear. In the second part, their partner will ask them questions without letting the first investigator know the question. Afterward, the data is analyzed in an attempt to find correlations in responses. Developers feel that the white noise created by the spirit box combined with the deprivation methods lulls the investigator into a trance-like state, enabling the spirit world to communicate. This method has been especially successful when the investigator is someone who is empathic or psychic.

In addition to the use of electronic and mechanical devices to detect the presence of ghosts and spirits, many investigators also incorporate their unique intuitive abilities, which they feel helps them find and communicate with the spirit world. These include empathic abilities, mediumship abilities, psychic communication and other empirical methods such as scrying, dowsing, clairvoyance, clairaudience, clairsentience, mediumistic and other psychic means. Empaths, psychic mediums and those with clairvoyant abilities find these abilities extremely useful in connecting with the spirit realm. Scrying, the ancient art of revelation, is derived from the Old English word *descry* ("reveal"). It is usually done in an effort to learn things that are unknown or unseen. While scrying isn't a tool that can be used to predict the future, it is believed that the practitioner can tap into the unconscious and the collective consciousness of the cosmos. While the future can't be seen, scrying can seem future-oriented, because it can help one to re-center or re-focus their direction or life path. Mirror gazing is the most commonly practiced form of scrying, although some psychics use oil, crystals, water and wax, as well as looking into someone else's eyes. Perhaps this is the origins of the belief that the eyes are the window to the soul. In a typical session, the scryer enters a relaxed state, lets their mind wander and stares into a mirror. These meditative actions help them enter into a trancelike state. They will then use any images and scenes that come to them to interpret the message.

Empathy is the ability to be in tune with or resonate with others, which can either be involuntary or voluntary. Empaths act as a sort of "tuning fork" and can actually feel the emotions of the people around them. In the case of the departed, empaths attempt to communicate with spirits or pick up on the emotional energy of spirits held in buildings. Many empathetic people are not sure how or why they have this ability; they simply accept it as part of their unique makeup. Empathic or psychic mediums can often "feel" the emotions of the spirits, such as sadness or despair, as if it were actually happening to them. Most empaths, aware that they may encounter energies that may be negative or draining, protect themselves by a variety of methods, including meditation, prayer or crystals, as well as keeping a positive attitude. A few gifted mental mediums say they can actually see the form of the spirit. Numerous investigators have related stories of being the recipients of mischievous or impish pranks, such as being touched, poked, nudged, pinched or having their hair pulled by unseen forces. Some empathic investigators believe these sometimes unnerving outward manifestations are due to the spirits' desire to be acknowledged and are not malicious or harmful.

Mediums use their abilities to act as messengers between two worlds, that of the living and that of the spirits. With this ability, they feel they are able to move through the veil between the two worlds and to communicate with, and relay messages from, the spirit realm. A physical medium is said to be able to materialize objects seemingly out of thin air. While extremely rare, a few physical mediums claim the ability to manifest the spirits themselves, often producing them through a substance called ectoplasm. The spirits can also manifest by producing sounds such as knocking, rapping on tables and ringing bells. This spectral activity was a well-known feature of séances, although many of the instances occurring during the heyday of spiritualism proved to be hoaxes. Some physical mediums will also allow the spirit to control their bodies in order to enable the spirit to speak directly to the living. A mental medium can communicate with those who have passed on by the use of telepathy. They "hear" the spirits through the use of clairaudience, or "see" them in the mind's eye through clairvoyance, as if they were images projected onto a screen or a photograph. Mediums with clairaudience abilities can channel or hear spirits' voices, similar to hearing a living person speak. Other mediums say they hear them more as a verbal thought. A more problematic type of mediumship ability comes in the form of "clairsentience." This is the taking on of an illness or physical problem of the spirit that they had in life or that was the cause of their death. This has also been referred to as "ghost sickness" and can have dire consequences for an investigator with clairsentience abilities unless they employ methods to protect themselves. To prevent absorbing any negative energies or taking on any thought forms emanating from the spirit world, before entering a building or area that is reputed to be haunted, investigators often employ a variety of methods. Some recite prayers, conduct meditation or use crystals, energized stones or incense as a means of protection. Even so, some ghost hunters report that after their encounters, they will have to cleanse and "recharge" for a time.

Ghost sickness is the belief that a ghost or spirit can harm the living or make them ill or even cause death. While this belief is not well known in modern western cultures outside of mainstream circles, historically, it is cross-cultural. Many of the indigenous people of the United States, including the Navaho and Lakota tribes, believed that ghost sickness was caused when a living person's thoughts became connected with the spirit's thoughts or behavior. The first manifestation of the sickness was an overwhelming sense of fear that followed them wherever they went. The fear was then accompanied by nightmares in which the deceased relayed messages to them, sometimes even attempting to entreat the person— usually a relative or loved one—to join them in the world of the dead. The symptoms of ghost sickness are said to range from headaches, nausea or weakness, to feelings of suffocation and terror, experiencing nightmares or dreaming of the departed. Other manifestations are a sense of dread, catatonic depression or hallucinations. These illnesses were not believed to be caused by anything natural but instead were supernatural in origin. In Native American and other cultures where this belief is still prevalent, these symptoms are usually relieved by naturopathic or shamanistic methods. Typical treatments include cleansing and purification of both the affected person and the dwelling and burning sage or other herbs to "chase" the spirits away. Ceremonies, chanting and rituals are also used in the belief that it will send the spirit back to the other realm. Current mainstream medicine attributes ghost sickness to grief experienced by family members for a loved one and employs traditional western medical and psychological therapies and modalities.

What are these brave and inquisitive investigators looking for when they venture into the dark and gloomy recesses of a supposed haunted building? Evidence, of course. This evidence can take on any number of paranormal manifestations that they believe indicates the presence of a spirit or haunting. Of course, one of the best and probably most startling kinds of evidence of a spirit manifestation is the sighting, either visually or on film, of a full-form apparition. As thrilling as that can be, it then needs to be determined if the apparition is of a dead person. There is some confusion as to the nature of apparitions. Most people automatically assume they are spirits of the dead, but that isn't always the case. An apparition is typically that of a living person. In fact, most reported apparitions tend to fall into this category. By definition, they are a person, thing or animal that is seen, felt or heard by supernatural means. They may commonly resemble human forms, although many also take on the forms of animals or other entities. They can also appear fog-like, silver, transparent or misty; can manifest with peculiar noises, smells or cold air; and can move objects, turn lights on and off and open and close doors and windows. It seems that stories about ghosts always involve dark, gloomy or stormy nights, and there may be some truth to it. Ghosts or apparitions are often seen under foggy or misty conditions or during thunderstorms. It is theorized that atmospheric conditions may play some part in this. They are also seen more frequently at night, perhaps because people maybe are more conducive to clairvoyant ability when relaxed or tired. Thus, the oft-used plot line of a frightening apparition accosting someone walking along a dark, lonely road on a foggy night is not just an overused cliché. This is something to remember the next time you are walking by a graveyard containing a newly dug grave.

Despite the fact that most apparitions are of the living, some of them are of the dead. Indeed, some of the most common apparitions reported are of the dead. These are most often seen or experienced soon after the person has died, either to comfort loved ones or to relay information. These are what we ordinarily refer to as ghosts, but the terms are often interchangeable. The ancients described ghosts as being disembodied souls that have traveled to the underworld. Belief that the spirits of the dead can return to haunt the living was an idea held by ancient Hebrews, Greeks and Romans. In fact, the majority of the world's cultures hold some belief in ghosts. In the Dark Ages, belief in apparitions, vampires, devil dogs and demons was commonplace. While belief in ghosts declined in the eighteenth century, it was revitalized in the nineteenth century in the form of spiritualism and its focus on the belief in survival after death. Along with this focus came increased interest in contact with the dead through mediumistic means. The study of apparitions, ghosts and spirits began in earnest in the late nineteenth century with the Society for Psychical Research. While cultures differ in their beliefs about what happens after death, most cultures believe that a ghost can return to the world of the living, with either good or bad intent. In western cultures, it is most commonly believed that a ghost is the soul of the deceased who cannot find peace or does not know they are dead, leading them to haunt the places where they lived or died. It may be that they have unfinished business on the earthly plane, perhaps to protect a loved one, impart information or reenact the death. Most of us are familiar with the ghost of Jacob Marley and his need to warn Ebenezer Scrooge to mend his ways in Charles Dickens's classic tale *A Christmas Carol*. An apparition's unfinished business can be of the collective, crisis or deathbed variety. A collective apparition is a manifestation of either the living or the dead to multiple witnesses. A crisis apparition is an image that appears in a moment of crisis to warn of danger or impending death. A deathbed apparition is a visual image of a divine being, religious figure or dead loved one seen by the dying.

Several theories have been proposed to explain apparitions. Some theories may shed light on the subject, but none go so far as to explain the different types and manifestations. Early researchers explained apparitions as hallucinations, some form of telepathy or mental projections. Recently, other theories have been advanced, including the belief that they are idea patterns produced by the subconscious, astral bodies, personality patterns trapped in the psychic field, thought forms, imprints of vibrations impressed upon some type of psychic ether or true spirits of the dead. None of these, however, is felt to be comprehensive enough to explain all apparitions in all instances. It is possible that some may be caused by the living, some may have their own reality and others may be caused by hallucinations or misidentification of natural phenomena. Still others may be the result of psychic recordings. Any and all of these manifestations may overlap at other times, with some elements of each being present to some degree.

A more difficult and perhaps downright frightening aspect of having a ghost about is when they cause trouble. Luckily, this is not a problem most people have to worry about. Some people may even enjoy the idea of having a spirit present. Although, if you've moved into a haunted house and made friends with the resident ghost, you may want to mention this before you send out the house-warming invites, especially if your ghost friend likes to act up. One of the ways that ghosts can become troublesome is when they attach themselves to a living person. Spiritual attachment is a form of possession whereby a discarnate entity attaches itself to a living person, usually due to some form of confusion on the part of the spirit. Those who work with spirit possession or attachments have identified symptoms including depression, mood swings, multiple personality disorder or sudden changes in behavior. The symptoms may vary depending on the degree of attachment, and it is theorized that if a spirit is benign, a person may not be aware of the attachment. Modern spirit workers use a variety of methods to get the spirit to leave the person, including exorcism and prayer. The first person to approach the idea of spiritual attachment was American physician Carl Wickland, who used electric shock treatments in order to release them from a patient's aura. These reports have apparently increased since the late 1980s. Attachment is believed to happen when a person dies but, for some reason, the spirit feels it has unfinished business on earth. They get "stuck" on this plane and may randomly attach themselves to a human. Unfortunately, the living can become more vulnerable to such attachments if they consume alcohol, use drugs, have suffered a traumatic accident or have undergone major surgery involving the use of anesthesia. Being close to a dying person may also make a person more susceptible to spiritual attachment, as the spirit will look for a new host. Some attachments may also be karmic in nature; unless the spirit is released, it can stay attached for the life of the host.

While the belief in ghosts has been with us for hundreds if not thousands of years, not everyone ascribes to this belief. Disbelievers usually explain away any and all reports of ghosts, apparitions and hauntings by way of hallucinations, psychological factors, misidentification of natural phenomena or hoaxes. The founder of the Society for Psychical Research, Frederick Myers, felt that ghosts were a manifestation of personal energy that persists or a similar force that is applied after death that is somehow connected to the person when alive. Modern paranormal investigators admit that many reported cases can be explained by natural means, but there are still a number that cannot. These cases make up about 2 percent. That is not a large number, but it is entirely possible that Muskegon, Michigan, has some mysterious places that might count among that 2 percent. Let's take a look at Muskegon's haunted past with thirteen of its eeriest stories, along with some of their real-life investigations.

1

EIGHTEEN ROSES FOR ANNIE

GHOSTS OF HUME HOUSE

*Thou know'st 'tis common, that all that lives must die /
Passing through nature to eternity.*
—Hamlet, *William Shakespeare*

In an upstairs window, a curtain moves in Hume House. The ethereal figure of a young girl looks down forlornly at the tourists below in the courtyard. Her soulful eyes watch silently. She longs to be able to walk among them, but she cannot. This isn't because she is being held prisoner, like some fairytale princess. It is because she is not a living person at all, but a spirit—one of them—said to haunt this Victorian-era home in Muskegon, Michigan. Hume House is a familiar symbol from Muskegon's lumber days and is now part of a museum complex. Many people are familiar with the rumor that it is haunted, and a number of ghost stories surrounding it have been told for years. Most of the stories say it is either Annie or Margaret Hume whose spirit has never left. Before it was a local historical site, the Hume House was built by Thomas Hume, a prominent lumber baron, to be the family home. Thomas Hume was born on June 14, 1848, in County Down, Ireland, the oldest of eight children. Hume immigrated to the United States after having served for a time as an apprentice at the tender age of fourteen. He eventually landed in Marshall, Michigan, to stay with relatives. A few years later, he came to Muskegon after being told that men were desperately needed and that work was plentiful. Soon after arriving, he joined Charles Hackley's lumber company as a bookkeeper. He and Hackley became business partners in 1881, creating the lumber firm Hackley and Hume. In its heyday, the company had the distinction of being second to none in the country for lumber production. At one time, the firm held over three hundred thousand acres of prime timberland in Louisiana, Mississippi, Arkansas and South Carolina, as well as a large manufacturing facility in Muskegon. Hackley and Hume were also stockholders in the Itasca Lumber Company in Minneapolis, Minnesota. Thomas held various offices within this company, including president. He was also president of the Amazon Knitting Company, the Chase-Hackley Piano Company, the Alaska Refrigerator Company and many others. Charles purchased a series of lots on Webster and Sixth Streets and began construction on a house. He then divided the lots and sold half to Thomas Hume. Hume and Hackley were not only business partners, they were also friends, so it seemed natural for them to want to also be neighbors. Thus, Hume began construction of a house on the lot next to Hackley's. It was a plan that worked out well for everyone, as the families lived there throughout their lives. Hume married Margaret Banks, daughter of Major Banks of Marshall, Michigan. They had seven children: Tom Junior, Nick (Tim), Helen, Annie Eliza, George, Florence and Constance. The Hume family and several live-in servants were the only people who ever lived in the house.

In addition to the two homes, a carriage house was built to accommodate a carriage, horses and livery drivers. Use of the carriage house was divided between the Hackley and Hume families, right down to having a dividing wall between the two halves and with the unique feature of having steeples that matched each house. While curious things were said to happen in the Hume residence, some pretty strange stories were also told about the carriage house, which is now known as the City Barn. It was built at the same time as the houses on their adjacent lots. There were four coachmen, two for each family. Their quarters were on the second level, which overlooked the courtyard between the two houses. They had their own separate entrances. The entrance to the carriage house was through an alley that led to the courtyard with large doors at the ends. Feed for the horses was once kept on the top floor. There was also storage space and a turret room for each coachman. The floor is now used as an area for exhibits and offices. When the families lived in the homes, the barn had a radiator on which the family and livery drivers would hang their damp clothing and woolen mittens. Oddly, even though it has been over one hundred years since anyone had mittens that needed drying, the dank, musty odor of wool drifts through the barn on occasion, without a wet mitten or long drawers in sight. The carriages and

Above: Hume House, Hackley-Hume Historic Site. *Illustration by ©Gabe Schillman, www.studio37arts.com. 2022. Newaygo, Michigan.*

Right: Thomas Hume. Print, 1913. *Jack Studio, Hume Family Collection, Lakeshore Museum Center, Muskegon, Michigan.*

Thomas Hume

horses belonging to each family were on the ground level. The barns have been thoroughly cleaned, renovated and painted. And while the horses are long gone, as are their droppings, staff and visitors have often experienced the distinctive odor of horse manure assail their noses as it wafted through the building. It wouldn't be at all unusual to smell horse manure if you had a stable full of horses. It would pretty much guarantee that the pungent smell of manure would be nearby, especially in humid weather. But it is unusual for that odor to still be present a century and a half after the last horse left. Granted, horse manure has a pungent odor, but after a hundred years or so, it surely would have dissipated. The smell is said to be so strong that visitors seem sure they have stepped in it. This is one instance in which visitors are glad there is no physical manifestation. Ectoplasmic manure is probably a lot easier to remove from one's shoes.

Hume House is an iconic symbol of the Victorian era's wealth and style. It was built using a design ordered from a pattern book, with David S. Hopkins as the architect. During the latter part of the nineteenth century, these preset house designs came into vogue, some simple and utilitarian, others with turrets and extravagant architecture, as in the case of the Hackley House. Both houses on the Hackley-Hume site were constructed at the same time using the same carpenters and workers. While very similar to the Hackley House in basic style, Hume's was built to accommodate a larger family. Thus it was not as elaborate in design or grandeur, which seemed fitting, as Hume was a junior partner in the firm, with Hackley owning three-quarters of the business. Victorian houses generally had two parlors. The first was a formal living room used for special occasions or parties. The second was for day-to-day family use or informal get-togethers. This was where the family could unwind, talk of the news of the day and drink cocoa by the fire. Victorian houses were known for having whimsical turrets as well as wrap-around porches, where the family could be seen sipping lemonade and visiting with friends and neighbors.

The Hume House, while not as ornate and expensive as the Hackley House, was made in the Queen Anne style. This style was the height of fashion through the late 1800s and became widely available and popular among the wealthy. Of all the splendid houses built during the Victorian age by those who could afford them, those in the Queen Anne style stand out as the most extravagant, as well as the most unconventional. While it is looked on with a romantic tint today, the industrial age in which these homes thrived was the antithesis of romance. While easily recognizable, the uniqueness of the Queen Anne style is still difficult to define. Some have

Hackley-Hume Historic Site, Lakeshore Museum Center.

turrets, some don't. They can resemble a gingerbread house or be made entirely of bricks. The Hume House was completed in 1888 with a library and a dining room, as well as a formal parlor. A sleeping porch was added after the turn of the century. After no longer functioning as a family home, it served as the local American Red Cross office before being obtained by the Heritage Group. This group, with the assistance of others in the community, restored the house to its previous glory as one of the best representatives of Queen Anne architecture in the United States. Eventually, it became part of the Lakeshore Museum, along with the Hackley House and City Barn, and was opened to the public for tours. Many of the family's artifacts and original furniture have been preserved. The site hosts thousands of visitors every year.

Throughout the years, there have been many rumors of strange and unexplainable events at the house, from objects and furniture being moved, the sound of mysterious footsteps and the inexplicable smell of roses. Alarms have been known to go off with no intruders being present—no living ones, at least—beds being unmade and food being moved around in the refrigerator. Some rooms have experienced

Main hallway of Hume House, Hackley-Hume Historic Site. Lakeshore Museum Center.

marked differences in temperature. Several of the back rooms, which had previously been servants' quarters, are often noted to be markedly colder. A floral scent has been prominent in several of the rooms on occasion, most notably near Margaret Hume's bedroom. A few visitors claimed to have encountered several ghosts at the house. Several people have seen a person pull back the curtain and gloomily peer down at them from an upstairs window, even though there should have been no one up there, as the site was closed for the season. Another person saw an apparition of a young girl in the same room with them during a guided tour. The scent of roses with no flowers present, the sound of footsteps when no one is around and the appearance of ghostly figures would certainly pique the interest of ghost hunters. One thing investigators might want to know during an investigation is if anyone died in the home and, if so, how. At the Hume House, there were multiple deaths and funerals of family members, including four deaths from natural causes. At least two funerals were held there. Thomas Hume died from pneumonia in the first-floor bedroom on December 31, 1919, at the age of seventy-one. The funeral of Thomas's younger brother, Abraham Hume, was held in 1899, and Florence Hume's funeral was held in 1920, both in the first parlor. Florence's husband and daughter lived in the house after she died. A lock of Florence's hair, along with a photo of Margaret and her daughter, sit on a dresser. Margaret Hume died at the age of ninety-five on August 30, 1943, in the master bedroom. Helen Hume was seventy-four years old when she died in her room on December 19, 1949.

WHEN SOMEONE RELATES A story of a strange or unusual occurrence, the mind of the listener seeks to find a cause. The stories of inexplicable footsteps, strange odors and apparitions, if taken at face value, have the earmarks of a haunting or attachment, although there may very well be rational explanations for everything said to have been experienced here. To ghost investigators, these unusual occurrences—especially seeing apparitions— offer a strong indication of something paranormal happening. In fact, the accounts might really get them excited, because they seem to have all the indicators of a haunted house. But if the home is indeed haunted, whose ghost or ghosts might they be? Are the footsteps the spirit of Mr. Hume as he contemplates his business ventures? Or are they the sounds of ghost horses in the carriage house? The floral scent experienced by visitors and staff near the bedrooms could be the spirit of Margaret putting roses in Annie Hume's bedroom. Annie "Nannie" Hume was only seventeen when she died on August 17, 1894, in her room. In remembrance of her, her mother put eighteen pink roses in her room every year. Margaret never failed to remember her daughter's birthday in this way. It was a birthday her beloved daughter never got to see. It could be the spirit of Annie Eliza

Hume House turret window. Curtains are seen moving in upstairs bedrooms. The ghostly figure of a young female stands in the window.

peering from behind a curtain in an upstairs window. Annie was quite frail and sick for most of her life, a result of heart and spinal problems, so she rarely left her room. One can easily feel sympathy for the frail girl destined to spend most of her life confined to her bedroom, unable to join her siblings in childhood games or the rambunctious antics that a house full of children would entail. One can imagine that Annie in all probability had spent her life being an onlooker to most of the family's day-to-day life. She was likely not able to withstand much of the excitement involved in events or holidays. It is entirely fathomable to picture her ghost longing for such family interaction and connection, not aware that she has passed on. Such energy is said to linger even after the people are no longer present. While the deaths in the house were not traumatic or violent, there is still the heartbreak, as in the untimely death of Annie Eliza and the grieving of her mother, who never fully got over her daughter's death. That Annie was not able to live a full life due to sickness is quite tragic. One can imagine that she often felt lonely and sad, but the Hume House, in its time, was a home in every sense of the word, with much family goings-on of one sort or another. This was a house filled with children, love and laughter, as well as roses for Annie.

2

SWEEPING SPIRITS
AND PHANTOM FOOTSTEPS

GHOSTS OF HACKLEY HOUSE

In an upstairs room, a maid diligently sweeps, her broom swishing away the dust. Downstairs, a man walks through the house as he goes about the business of running a home, his footsteps on the wood floors echoing throughout. The strange thing is, there are no maids to sweep and no one should be walking about. No one lives here. This is Hackley House, where some unsettling things are said to happen on occasion. It seems that the Hume House is not the only place where a few strange things are said to go on. Perhaps it is because, like the Hume House, the Hackley family home is old, well over one hundred years old. As anyone who loves ghost stories knows, old houses tend to get this sort of reputation. Even so, some of these stories are indeed curious—some would say downright creepy.

The house was the residence of lumber baron and philanthropist Charles Hackley, his wife, Julia, and their adopted children, Charles Moore and Erie. Julia Esther Moore was twenty-six when she married Charles Hackley in 1864. Julia died in 1905 at the age of sixty-six after a long illness. Hackley and Hume had been neighbors on Webster Avenue. Both houses occupy a set of lots formerly owned by Alexander Rogers. The site was picked for its amenities, such as light, heating and sewer systems. Hackley bought all three lots in 1887. Hume purchased a lot from Hackley, and they built a carriage house on the third lot, which they shared. That structure is now known as the City Barn. The houses were some distance from what was considered downtown and a ways from Hackley's lumber mill office on Western Avenue. This house is also in the Queen Anne style, like the Hume House, with the biggest differences being the cost and the grandeur. Hackley's house was custom-built by architect David Hopkins, costing upward of $50,000, a large sum for the time (today, more than $1,400,000). It was completed in two years, along with the Hume House and carriage house.

The Hackley House is an example of Queen Anne architecture unparalleled in Michigan and is an impressive sight to behold. Queen Anne houses were typically painted colorfully. The Hackley House is no exception; thirteen different colors were used on the home. With its gabled roof, towering spindles, corner tower and colorfully painted shingles that have been painstakingly restored, one has the sense of looking back in time. As far as architecture goes, this house is unique, combining a wide array of decoration. Lacy spindles, classical columns, arched windows, elaborate moldings and stained glass were all united, creating the sense of wealth and elegance that many lumber barons were keen to display. The home's interior is equally imposing and breathtakingly beautiful. The house is known for the beautifully carved wood staircases and moldings depicting mythical beasts and animals. The intricately carved cherry, oak and butternut woodwork is prominent throughout. Some of the walls have hand-stenciled designs and immense, elaborate fireplaces. Radiant stained-glass windows cast mesmerizing rays of color throughout. These unique and beautiful windows stand as one of the house's great achievements and are priceless. While different companies were used for the windows, floors, wood carvings and fireplace, they were incorporated to create a house that is both magnificent and iconic. The Hackley family moved into the house in 1889, around the same time as the Hume family did in their residence.

Of the many historical figures prominent in the Muskegon area, Charles Hackley stands out as the most iconic and most familiar, with a life story that could rival the best rags-to-riches novel. When Charles came to Muskegon as a young man seeking his fortune, it was said he had only a few dollars in his pocket. When he died in 1905, his estate was valued at $12 million, having endowed over $6 million to the City of Muskegon. Charles was Muskegon's most devoted advocate. Through his efforts and those of several other lumber barons, Muskegon successfully transitioned from a stagnating lumber community to a city with rapidly growing potential and a diverse industrial base.

Charles Henry Hackley was born in Michigan City, Indiana, on January 3, 1837. His family moved to Wisconsin while he was still a small child. As a youth, Charles worked in addition to attending school, but he left school at the age of fifteen to work with his father. His drive for success was evident at

Carriage and horses, Hackley House, circa 1890s. Hackley-Hume Historic Site, Lakeshore Museum Center. *Muskegon Picture Collection; Local History & Genealogy Department, Hackley Public Library, Muskegon, Michigan.*

an early age, and at sixteen, he was put in charge of a small crew that repaired and maintained roads. When the senior Hackley could not find work as a carpenter, he made his way to Michigan to work in the lumber industry, which was still in its early stages. Charles soon joined his father, coming to Michigan in 1856 on the schooner *Challenge*. He was soon employed at Durkee, Truesdell and Company as a day laborer making twenty-two dollars a month, a good wage at that time. After the mill closed, he began work as a scaler, which enabled him to learn the lumber business and discover its potential as a profitable industry. After spending the winter in the Michigan wilderness, he began work as a foreman at a mill. When that mill closed due to lack of business in the economic slump of 1857, he decided to return to school for business training, traveling to Kenosha. Diploma in hand, he returned to Muskegon and was made a bookkeeper at Durkee, Truesdell and Company. He was an avid learner, and his knowledge of the lumber industry continued to grow. He also had a sharp eye for marketing and industry possibilities. He soon understood that lumber would be vital for the growth of the United States and that Michigan could play an integral part

Right: Portrait of Julia Hackley. Hackley-Hume Historic Site, Lakeshore Museum Center. *Painted by Edwin E. Turner, circa 1890.*

Below: Antique carriage. Hackley-Hume Historic Site, Lakeshore Museum Center.

CHARLES H. HACKLEY

1837 – 1905

LUMBER BARON, WHO APPLIED HIS FORTUNE DURING HIS
LIFETIME TO CREATE A CITY OF DISTINCTION. HIS GIFTS
INCLUDED A LIBRARY, HOSPITAL AND ART MUSEUM OF THE
HIGHEST QUALITY, THE FIRST KINDERGARTEN AND THE FIRST
MANUAL TRAINING SCHOOL IN THE STATE OF MICHIGAN,
AND THE PARK TOWARD WHICH HIS BRONZE NOW GAZES.

"I consider that a rich man to a great extent owes his fortune to the public."
– C. H. Hackley, August 18, 1900

Sculptor: William F. Duffy   The Large Art Company

Presented to the community by Peter M. Turner, Sr.
2009

Plaque commemorating philanthropy of Charles Hackley, Baker College Culinary Institute of Michigan.

in it. At age twenty-two, Charles, along with his father and Mr. Truesdell, purchased the property of Pomeroy and Holmes, thus forming the J.H. Hackley Company. The company was successful and expanded, purchasing another mill. Charles was the bookkeeper for both companies as well as for Mr. Truesdell.

Not content with the status quo, Charles continued to invest in and buy mills. When James McGorden purchased the senior Hackley's share of the Wing Mill, Hackley went into business with McGordon. Unfortunately, the Wing mill was destroyed in a fire and was not rebuilt. Hackley soon formed C.H. Hackley and Company with McGordon. Thomas Hume came on as a bookkeeper and a shareholder, and the men eventually formed the Hackley and Hume Company and created one of the largest lumber mills in the nation. They would remain partners, as well as friends, throughout Hackley's lifetime. The company ceased operations in 1894. With the speed at which the timber was being harvested, it was inevitable that the lumber boom would end just as quickly. By the late 1800s, Michigan's forests were all but gone. Muskegon had forty-seven sawmills and was entirely dependent on the mills and the income it brought. In 1891, a fire wiped out the majority of the business district, leaving many mills in ruins and people homeless. To add insult to injury, the United States

Left: Statue of seated Charles Hackley. Baker College Culinary Institute of Michigan. *Sculpted by Bill Duff, 2009.*

Below: Hackley Administration building.

was undergoing a financial crisis. Relying predominantly on the lumber industry, Muskegon was hit hard by all of this. These disasters brought many people to the brink, and many were left homeless.

Charles and other mill owners were heavily invested in the mills and in the city. They realized that in order to survive, they needed to find a way to breathe life back into the economy. Some companies began by finding viable options, diversifying into lumber-related products such as curtain rollers, packaging and furniture. The Chase Piano Company, Amazon Knitting, Continental Motors and Central Paper Company, as well as many others, were founded by 1897. With the changing economic climate, many of the mill owners became involved in city and local politics. A good number of Muskegon's mayors in the late 1800s were associated with the lumber industry. Charles Hackley ran for mayor himself several times and served as alderman, treasurer and on the school board. He was also a state delegate to the National Republican Convention on several occasions. Knowing that education was vital, Charles gifted funds to build a training school, with an additional endowment of $100,000 for its continued upkeep and teachers' salaries. The training center was eventually expanded to several more buildings as enrollment increased. Charles was a significant benefactor to the city, giving millions to its betterment and upkeep. He believed in the ideas in Dale Carnegie's 1889 treatise, "The Gospel of Wealth," whereby those who are able to, should give back to alleviate hardship as well as invest in those who wish to improve their own lives by education and training. Charles is quoted as saying, "A rich man to a great extent owes his fortune to the public. He makes money largely through the labor of his employees….Moreover, I believe that it should be expended during the lifetime of the donor, so that he can see that his benefactions do not miscarry and are according to his intent….To a certain extent, I agree with Mr. Carnegie…that it is a crime to die rich."

Charles Hackley was still a prosperous man when he died, but he also made the city prosper. The gifts that Hackley gave to the city, if measured by the knowledge instilled in those who used the library, walked in the serenity of the tree-lined park, marveled at world-class art in the Hackley Art Gallery, or whose lives were saved at the hospital or benefited from the poor fund, cannot be adequately quantified. But if a monetary value is put on them, it amounts to over $6,000,000 by today's standards. His endowments include Hackley Public Library, Hackley Hospital and Nursing School, Soldiers' Monuments at Hackley Park, Hackley Art Gallery, Hackley Park, Hackley Training School and Gymnasium and Hackley Athletic Field. One of his first donations was $150,000 to purchase art for the library. Originally, the art was to be housed at the library, but after that venue was determined to be unsuitable, the Hackley Art Gallery was established. The cornerstone of the art gallery was laid in October 1911, and the facility opened in 1912. At the time, the gallery was considered to be the first of importance for a city the size of Muskegon, and it continues to be a world-class venue.

The last of the Hackley family moved away in 1920. Erie Hackley, their adopted daughter, was the last person to live in the home. She then rented out the house, first to Robert Bunker, then to the Jones family. Eventually, Erie gave the house to the Red Cross, which occupied it for about twenty-five years. After the Red Cross left in 1962, both houses were vacant and fell into disrepair, to the point that they needed to be torn down. Luckily, they were saved when the Hackley Heritage Association worked to have the homes designated as historic buildings. This group later recruited the help of the Lakeshore Museum to continue the work. The houses became part of the Lakeshore Museum system, and restoration went into full swing. This restoration continues today.

WHILE THIS BEAUTIFULLY RESTORED icon of the Victorian age is magnificent in its architecture and opulence, it has also been described as disquieting and eerie. Perhaps it is because, although it was the Hackley family home for many years, it was also the place where a few people died. Just knowing that someone died in a house makes some people nervous, especially if they have heard that the home is haunted. When you throw a few autopsies into the mix, things get a little more unsettling. This may be the case with the Hackley House. It was the site of four deaths and four funerals, including those of Charles Hackley and Mary Ann Moore, Julia's mother. After suffering health issues, Charles went to Salt Lake City for treatment, but he passed away of an aneurysm after returning home. Charles was sixty-eight when he died in the first-floor bedroom. This room was used as a guest room and a sick room when the need arose. Julia also passed away there. The autopsies of Charles and Julia were done in the home, reportedly in the dining room. While some people feel this is all a bit too weird or morbid, others find it as thrilling and spine-tinglingly delightful as sitting by a roaring campfire and telling ghost stories. It may be those same thrill-seeking and curious folks who enjoy the annual Hackley-Hume House Tours, which are of the more shadowy kind, usually scheduled around Halloween. An Obituary Tour enthralls visitors with an in-depth look into Victorian death and dying practices as well as a discussion of the deaths, funerals and autopsies that occurred at both houses. Fright Night at the Museum promises a chillingly good time. Visitors are invited to spend a creepy evening finding their way through a spine-tingling maze. Another tour offered visitors the chance to find out for themselves if the ghost stories were true. That tour was done in the dark; visitors were armed only with flashlights.

Some stories told over the years include phantom footsteps heard by maintenance workers, even when the house was closed to visitors and other staff were gone for the day. The sound of people talking when no one else was around had also been noted. A few visitors to the house have described feeling as if someone was behind them, only to turn and find no one there. Murmuring sounds were heard coming from the attic, which at one time was used as a bedroom and a playroom. On another occasion, a mournful, wailing sound was heard coming from the attic. Workers have arrived in the morning, only to find trash piled in the middle of rooms. Food in the refrigerator would be shifted around. In the room that had formerly been used as a maid's quarters, a bed sometimes looked as if someone had been lying on it, including having an indentation on the pillow, even though it had been neatly made up the previous day. A chair in Julia's room would frequently be moved from one location to a position in front of the window. Windows that were always kept locked would be found unlocked; doors that had been closed the day before would be found open the next day. The smell of cigar smoke was frequently noted by both staff and visitors, although this was a nonsmoking site. Interestingly, the odor of cigars has also been noted in the Hackley Library, another building frequented by Mr. Hackley. In one disconcerting incident, a bathroom doorknob was said to be rattling as if someone on the other side was trying to open it, even though no one else was around. This bathroom is connected to the bedroom that had been converted into a sick room and where Charles Hackley spent his last days and died after contracting pneumonia. Julia had also used this bedroom. On a number of occasions, water could be heard running in an upstairs bathroom that was closed to tourists and was not used by staff. Objects in the house would turn up missing. Sometimes, they would be found in other rooms of the house.

Like many old houses, the Hackley House could seem a little eerie in the dark of night when no one was about. Museum staff would often be puzzled when objects turned up missing and were later found in different areas of the house, or when they would return in the morning to find some of the lights or fans on, sometimes even when they knew they had

Green man carving, Hackley House, Hackley-Hume Historic Site, Lakeshore Museum Center.

unplugged them the night before. Closet and outside doors that were always kept shut or locked would be found open. Windows that were kept locked would be found unlocked or open. Security alarms were said to go off inexplicably in the middle of the night or disarm and rearm themselves. After being thoroughly checked out by technicians, no cause could be found for this anomaly. Several photographs taken in the house purportedly show what appear to be white mists. One photo was said to have been taken in Julia's room, the other in Charles Hackley's library. Are these mists proof that the house is haunted, or do they indicate something else? Photographic evidence of apparitions is rare and, if genuine, would be compelling evidence for the reality of spirits. But there are other causes for the presence of mists, such as movement of the camera while the photo was being taken or photographic artifacts.

Except for a few instances, such as the alarms going off, these things are said to have occurred during the daytime. Despite the fact that a few people were put off by the stories and rumors of the area being haunted, no one had ever felt that anything negative or harmful was at the root of it. While an odd presence was sensed by a few people, no one has ever experienced being touched or harmed in any way. On the contrary, a few of those who believed in the hauntings would even "talk" to the spirits on occasion. A few of the Hackley family's possessions remain in the house on display, including Charles's glasses and pocket watch and Julia's umbrella, as well as numerous paintings of the family. These items give visitors a poignant look into Victorian family life. But from a paranormal perspective, they might also be a source for spiritual attachments. In addition, inexplicable odors can be an indication of paranormal activity. So, when one smells cigar or cigarette smoke when no one is about, it becomes a rather curious event.

These stories could easily be passed off as the result of misunderstandings or jittery nerves, but hearing discarnate voices, smelling strange odors and hearing the footsteps of an invisible person may be harder to ignore. The scent of cigars and the sounds in a locked attic and of phantom footsteps can be attributed to imprints left over in the house. But even with all of these curious events, the Hackley House is one of Muskegon's jewels. While a few people have felt unnerved by the rumors of ghosts, no one has reported feeling anything malevolent. The energy here is more akin to the spiritual presence of a family going about their lives. Charles and Julia were prominent residents of Muskegon, and they would no doubt have had people coming to call. Julia was community-minded and an active participant of many social groups. It is more than likely that the couple entertained many in their beautiful and opulent home. If there is some residual spiritual energy from a bygone era at the Hackley House, it might be the spirits of Charles and Julia letting people know they are still around. They may be pleased that people are still coming to call. Gracious Victorian hosts that they were, their spirits will want to make the house presentable for company, and the spectral maids will set to their job of sweeping up the phantom dust.

3

GRAMMA'S GHOST
IS BAKING COOKIES

GHOSTS OF TORRENT HOUSE

There is nothing like the warm, inviting aroma of freshly baked cookies, especially if they are baked by the loving hands of grandma. If their delightful fragrance meets your olfactory nerves, it's not long before you go in search of them. If you visit Torrent House in Muskegon and this scent greets you, you will be sorely disappointed if you seek out the cookies. There are no cookies and no baking grandma. There has been, however, the reported sighting of a grandma-like apparition, phantom footsteps, the sound of a crying child or baby and the scent of baking cookies. These cookies, if they existed, were gobbled up long ago. As one of Muskegon's most expensive homes, built during its lumber heyday, this Victorian mansion stands out as one with more than its share of stories surrounding it, including that of the paranormal kind. Torrent House is a thirty-one-room Richardsonian-style house located at 315 West Webster in Muskegon. It was designed and built by Johnson and Johnson Construction of Grand Rapids in 1891 for John and Caroline Torrent. This regal-looking building, with its grand turret and red-gabled roof, looks more like a medieval castle than a family home. At the time, it was the city's only residence made of stone. The interior of the house was just as lavish, finished throughout with mahogany, cherry, birch, pine, oak and redwood harvested from Michigan forests. Other imported materials were extensively used throughout. The Torrent House was the brainchild of lumbar baron John Torrent, one of Muskegon's most prominent and wealthy citizens.

Above: Torrent House, circa 1890s. The house originally had thirty-one rooms and was the most expensive house in town at the time. *Muskegon Picture Collection, Local History & Genealogy Department, Hackley Public Library, Muskegon, Michigan.*

Opposite: Stairwell at Torrent House. Local History & Genealogy Department, Hackley Public Library. Footsteps are often heard in upstairs rooms.

John was an entrepreneur, inventor, politician and real-estate mogul. Never willing to be outdone, he always did things on a grand scale. In fact, he seemed to be a master at one-upmanship, especially when it came to Charles Hackley. John Torrent and fellow lumber baron Charles Hackley were business rivals. So, when Hackley built his house, a Queen Anne–style mansion for a whopping $50,000, Torrent was determined to build an even grander home. To put it in perspective, Hackley's house would cost about $1,500,000 to build today. Torrent threw some heavy cash around, so to speak, giving Johnson and Johnson Construction what amounted to a blank check. With an unlimited budget, the firm estimated a price tag of around $100,000. Unfortunately, as construction progressed, design changes and problems with workers' unions ran up the cost. To add to the problems, when union bricklayers working on the house discovered that stonemasons working on a nearby school were nonunion, they

Above, left: Name plaque, Torrent House. Local History & Genealogy Department, Hackley Public Library.

Above, right: Fireplace, Torrent House. Local History & Genealogy Department, Hackley Public Library.

Opposite: Portrait of John Torrent. Local History & Genealogy Department, Hackley Public Library, Muskegon, Michigan. *Painting by L. Betts.*

went on strike. This snafu served to delay the work even further. If that wasn't bad enough, a fire broke out just before the house was completed, extensively damaging the lower portion of the building. There was no house insurance, so Torrent experienced more out-of-pocket costs to the tune of several thousand dollars. Ultimately, no doubt to the family's relief, the house was completed. By then, the massive stone structure reportedly cost $250,000 to build, an enormous sum of money. Today, a house of such design and materials would cost an astounding $6,500,000, if not more. The Torrent family moved into the house by the spring of 1894. The house was purchased by the City of Muskegon in 1972 to save it from demolition and is now listed as a historic building. In the years following the family's exit, the home has been used as a mortuary, a hospital and the area's Red Cross facility. Currently, it is part of the Hackley Library and houses genealogical and historical documents and information. It may have been John Torrent's drive to show up Charles Hackley at all costs, but a shadow seems to hang over the place. Some people think that Torrent's spirit is still there, as well as a few other ghosts.

John Torrent was likened to a Renaissance man. His wealth, power and influence were well known in Muskegon. He was a prominent figure in the community and held a variety of offices, including alderman, justice of the peace and three-time mayor. However, like many powerful and wealthy men of the day, even those who did much for their community, they can also be difficult to get along with. Judging by historical records, John Torrent had difficulties with many of his peers. He owned mills in Muskegon, Manistee, Ludington, Whitehall, Traverse City and Sault St. Marie. He was a shrewd

Torrent House. Local History & Genealogy Department, Hackley Public Library.

businessman and was able to achieve success by buying, building and selling lumber mills. Torrent seemed to have had a shark-like ability to turn a profit and a unique ability to know when to buy and when to sell. It was a skill that served him well, although it also caused him a few problems.

John Torrent was born in Watertown, New Jersey, in 1833, one of four children. The Torrent family moved to Canada, where John lived until the age of sixteen, when he decided to strike out on his own and moved back to the United States. Settling in Grand Haven, Michigan, he soon began working at the Ferry Mill. This was the beginning of Torrent's long career as a lumberman. He eventually held stock in numerous sawmills and other

Muskegon industries. His drive and ambition were there early on, and within a short time he was in charge of the entire mill. He came to Muskegon while still a young man and expected to stay on only a few months, but he decided to stay. He met and married Caroline Honner of Amherstburg, Ontario. He and Caroline had eight children.

He eventually opened up a shingle mill, which he later converted to a shingle- and sawmill. The shingle business was successful early on; the product was sold throughout the United States. In 1865, he built another mill, which he sold to his brother Esau Tarrent. He then purchased the George Arms Mill. He invested in two barges, the *R. McDonald* and the *Nellie Torrent*, in order to transport shingles and lumber. He also owned the *H.B. Moore*, a schooner. As successful as John Torrent was, intrigue and scandal seemed to follow him. One of the most notable scandals involved his rival, Charles Hackley. Hackley enlisted Torrent's help in buying land on which to place a park. In order to do so, Hackley needed the entire block. Torrent did as Hackley charged him to do, with one exception. Unbeknownst to Hackley, Torrent purchased the last two lots needed to complete the project at bargain prices, then turned around and tried to sell them to Hackley at double the price. It seemed he had Hackley over a barrel. Needless to say, Hackley was not happy and turned down the deal. The newspapers had a field day raking Torrent over the coals. Torrent and Hackley were at a stalemate for some time. Hackley even threatened to quash the whole project, but in time, the two men were able to come to an agreement. The park went on as planned.

To Torrent's peers and rivals, his business deals seemed ruthless. One thing was sure: he never pulled his punches or gave an inch if he could help it when it came to business. He was involved in numerous legal disputes throughout the years. At one time, he had simultaneous lawsuits against fourteen different companies for patent infringement, which he pursued aggressively. Torrent's brother Esau also owned a sawmill in Muskegon. In addition to being a rival with Charles Hackley, Torrent was pretty aggressive in quashing others who attempted to take over or start rival businesses. One such dispute was between log owners and one of Torrent's lumber companies. At one point, some log owners, deciding that the company's prices for sorting and delivering logs was too high, opted to start their own concern by dredging a new canal, apparently going through Torrent's property. This was promptly challenged by Torrent, who went to court and had a restraining order filed against them. After the enterprising log men managed to send a few hundred thousand logs downriver through their new route, Torrent had his foreman attempt to stop them by barring the way with a broomstick, with attorneys looking on. It was reported in the *Silver Standard* newspaper on June 22, 1895, that the tables were turned. The poor foreman was carried across the channel on the broomstick.

Torrent's disputes were not confined to rival companies. In the ten years he served as alderman for the city, he was involved in more scandals and intrigue, becoming entangled in a dispute with the city over a reimbursement on a device he had purchased. It seemed that Torrent wanted more than what he actually paid for the device. The city, of course, took issue with that request. The newspapers got wind of it and had a field day, leading to his being tried in the court of public opinion. Torrent was true to form, and when one newspaper smeared him, he quickly sued it for slander. He was never charged in the reimbursement fiasco but later resigned as alderman. Another incident had him allegedly attempting to take advantage of his political ties; at the very least, he was guilty of conflict of interest. This happened when he opened a saloon next door to his theater. The problem was, he was president of the Citizen's League at the same time. The league was responsible for cleaning up graft and other illegal activities in Muskegon. It was also charged with keeping a watchful eye on drinking by minors. It seemed that Torrent was trying to have his beer and drink it, too. He courted trouble, and it usually had a way of landing him in court. He became the focus of a tax-evasion scandal involving one of his lumber mills and tried to start a bank called the John Torrent. He was absolved of wrongdoing on the charge of tax evasion. Not surprisingly, his audacious bank scheme did not go over well with city leaders and business owners.

But for all his scandals and misdeeds with business rivals, Torrent seemed to fare better as Muskegon's mayor. He helped to bring about numerous positive changes and improvements to the city. One change concerned Muskegon's streets. While it is hard to imagine this being allowed today, at the time, it was common to see chickens, goats, horses, mules and cattle meandering along the city streets. Torrent was instrumental in passing an ordinance against this, one most likely applauded by the ladies, given the long dresses they wore. Talk about a laundry nightmare! Torrent also worked to improve Muskegon's water and sewer systems as well as the electrical grid. He advocated changes to the police and fire departments in order to make them better organized. He improved the dismal conditions at the local poorhouse, much to his credit. His financial escapades were often fodder for gossip, and he was frequently maligned by the press and convicted in the court of public opinion. But the work he did for the community showed a side of him that is often overlooked. Despite his negative image, he was a man of strong willpower and a pioneering spirit who did not easily back down. This strength of character saw him through the worst of times. In addition to the house that continues to be a marvel today, he left behind an extensive legacy of growth, enterprise and community work. John Torrent died in 1915 at the age of eighty-two in his home on Webster Avenue.

After the family no longer lived in the house, it was used first as a mortuary, then as a small private hospital. Muskegon Osteopathic Hospital began operating after a group of local physicians purchased the massive, thirty-one-room mansion. The initial opening was delayed when the current tenant, a local mortician, apparently refused to leave. After the mortuary left, the hospital installed twenty beds and equipment. The hospital opened its doors in 1942. Dr. John Wallace was one of the doctors in its first year of operation. After interning, Dr. Wallace served in a variety of technical positions, from performing X-rays to working in the lab, and even as a cook. Not long after his arrival, the inquisitive Wallace decided to explore the house. Opening a large drawer in the basement, he was surprised to find a decomposing body, inadvertently left behind by the mortician. The forgotten client was quickly retrieved by the mortician. If anyone had a right to haunt the place, it would have been that poor, forgotten soul. At first, the kitchen served as an operating room, as the tiled floors and walls were easier to clean. A new addition with three floors doubled the capacity of the hospital, with sixty-seven adult beds, eight pediatric beds and ten newborn beds. The emergency room was on the first level, as was the information center, supply rooms, surgical units and patient rooms. The second floor had twenty-four beds with two labor rooms and a delivery room. The lower level housed the laboratory, radiology department, cafeteria and kitchen. In the original building, there were administrative offices, a pharmacy, meeting rooms and maintenance facilities. There were twenty-five patient beds in ten rooms, including a pediatrics department with eight beds.

The Torrent House went from being the home of a rather stern lumber baron to a mortuary and then a hospital. So it made perfect sense that Kent County Paranormal was asked to conduct a paranormal investigation of the building. The results of the investigation were presented as a public "reveal" at Hackley Public Library during Halloween. Although investigators were unaware of any rumors of hauntings associated with the house, they felt that an investigation at a Muskegon location would be of interest to area residents. Dan Schmidt and Brandon Hoezee were part of the team that investigated. Dan, a pastor on the team, attempted scrying, but this was not something they normally did. Typical of many investigations, a "walk-

Left: Kitchen, Torrent House. Local History & Genealogy Department, Hackley Public Library. The kitchen served as a surgery room when the house was used as a hospital.

Below: Wardrobe, Torrent House. Local History & Genealogy Department, Hackley Public Library. This is not part of the original furniture. A scrying session with the wardrobe mirror yielded positive results.

around" was performed by Brandon to see if he felt any energies. It was said that people had experienced paranormal activity in a parlor located on the main floor. There is also a very large, ornate, mirrored cabinet on the main floor. It currently is behind the receptionist's desk and faces the main doors. This cabinet was not part of the original furniture, but because of its beauty, it was kept. A figure had reportedly been seen in this mirror. This is where Dan did a scrying session. The goal was to see if he could communicate with this spirit energy. He sat quietly in front of the mirror for a time. After a while, he recounted getting mental images of an open field, a small house and a tree. He then got images of a woman in the field. She looked at him and then began moving toward him. Staff members and guests to the house have seen the full-form apparition of an elderly woman sitting in a chair in the parlor. Dan said he felt a presence in the house almost the entire time he was there. Brandon saw a hunched-over form of a woman when he walked into the parlor and noticed the scent of fresh-baked cookies. They also picked up the smell of cigar smoke in the downstairs area, which they felt wasn't natural to the environment. As smoking is not allowed in the area, the odor is not likely to be the result of someone smoking in the building.

A psychic medium was also part of the investigation, and who also saw this spirit form. Phantom footsteps have also been heard going from the area where the elderly woman is seen sitting. The footsteps are then heard going down a hall to a small room that is currently being used as storage. Several of the stories also involve hearing odd noises and voices. The sound of a baby crying is said to be coming from a room that was known to have been a baby's room. Footsteps have been heard going into this room. Other spirit forms were seen going behind a bookcase in a different part of the house. The team was unable to correlate any of the activity to any specific historical event or person, and they were not aware of any specific instances of paranormal activity or haunting previous to the investigation. In fact, the house was officially not haunted, but after the investigation, it was felt that some paranormal activity had indeed been evident. The psychic believed he felt the spirit of a little girl in the upper level of the turret room. The ground level contains an archive room where guests may sit and read or do research. This circular room has several large windows overlooking the street. Investigators felt a sense of heaviness when they walked into the room. It wasn't long before they received a response from the spirit. This manifested in the form of a strong, swirling energy that was almost palpable. It was noted to be especially strong in the corner of the room and described as a sort of psychic tornado. After the psychic connected with the little girl's

Left: Storage room, Torrent House. Local History & Genealogy Department, Hackley Public Library.

Right: Storage room and library, Torrent House. Local History & Genealogy Department, Hackley Public Library. Footsteps have been heard, and an apparition has been seen disappearing into the storage room.

spirit, the swirling energy field was felt by four members of the paranormal team as well as three staff members who were also in the room at the time.

The presence of an adult male was also sensed in the same area. The psychic got the sense that this man was trying to comfort or help the little girl in some way. He did not get the sense that there was any negative energy from this spirit. The investigators then went to the basement, where they picked up on some rather mystifying energy. The basement used to house a small surgery room and a morgue. Footsteps were heard along the back wall, and a discarnate voice told them to "come here." But if the investigators headed toward where they thought the voice was coming from, no one was there. They attempted to communicate with whatever or whoever was in the basement, but no clear EVP could be produced. Luckily, they were able to record footsteps on EVP devices. While they were downstairs, they heard footsteps upstairs. Brandon ran up to see if anyone was there and did another quick walk-through, trying to pinpoint the direction of the sounds. They seemed to be coming from the same area where the elderly lady spirit had been seen. At one point during the investigation, they picked up the name

Left: Archive room, Torrent House. Local History & Genealogy Department, Hackley Public Library.

Right: Turret room, Torrent House. Local History & Genealogy Department, Hackley Public Library. Whirling spirit energy is felt by investigators in the upper level of the turret room.

"Jessica" on EVP. They asked the staff if they were familiar with the name, but no one knew of any person with that name having worked there. Because so many people have come and gone through the Torrent House doors, it would be almost impossible to accurately pinpoint the identity of "Jessica." It is not believed that Jessica was anyone in the Torrent family. Other responses picked up on EVP were "no," which is common in such investigations. After John Torrent and his family had moved out of the residence, it saw many others passing through its halls—some living, some deceased.

The paranormal investigation team picked up some pretty intriguing evidence that may indicate that the Torrent House has more than a few ghosts. However, these ghosts or imprints do not seem to be frightening. On the contrary, it is rather uplifting to think that, however many enemies John Torrent made, the energies left in the house are positive. The grandmotherly apparition, phantom footsteps, whirling childlike energy and the ethereal sound of a crying baby may be imprints of a house where children played, were comforted when they cried and had a grandma who baked them cookies.

4

CLEAN-UP CREW GETS A CURIOUS TIP

GHOST OF DIVISION STREET

Cleaning up after someone is often a thankless job. Doing that job when a ghost is watching your every move can be unnerving to say the least. But in this case, it didn't go unrewarded. Some of the ways ghosts show their displeasure with people coming in or changing things around on them can be frightening, even dangerous. Because when a ghost is upset, they're going to let someone know about it, and not always in a nice way. It is usually those living in the home, friends or visitors who bear the brunt of their disapproval. If the house undergoes renovations, construction workers or home improvement personnel may also feel their discontent. There is at least one home in the Nims neighborhood where a cleanup crew caused a bit of annoyance for a ghost. Luckily, a little practical intervention by one of the workers, who instinctively understood they were probably dealing with something out of the ordinary, may have prevented things from taking a menacing turn. This story was related to me by a friend who worked for a preservation company. These companies subcontract to a bank or mortgage company and go in and make repairs or renovations after a house has been repossessed and vacated. The preservationist crew goes in and cleans up, reports any issues and makes repairs in order to bring a property up to code. For this story, the names have been changed for privacy reasons.

Spectral visions of wraithlike shadows passing through the walls of a Victorian manor, creating a disturbance or doing other unsettling things to the living, are the mainstay of Hollywood horror films and countless Gothic novels. If you have an aging, run-down house, you can almost bet that someone will wonder if it is haunted. But it isn't just those creepy old houses that are haunted. Many newer homes have been subject to paranormal energy and spirit manifestation. The causes in newer homes are basically the same as for older ones, such as tragic or sudden deaths or some sort of stored or imprinted energy.

Many times, the stimulus for things to start going bump in the night is when a house is remodeled, renovated or undergoes major repairs. Of course, any home, new or old, may need some renovation or maintenance from time to time to keep them from falling into disrepair. When structural upkeep or maintenance upsets a ghost's daily routine, things are bound to go south in a hurry. It's normal for people to get a little out of sorts when things change, so it should come as no surprise to hear that the departed can also get a little testy at this. Their annoyance can lead them to act out in a variety of ways, most notably attachment, possessiveness, confusion, spite and even anger. The difference is that people have the understanding and ability to adapt to the changes, whereas a ghost may not. They remain fixated and stuck in the same patterns, which might cause them to go bump in the night or perform other activities initiated by their confusion. Imagine going into a place where you have been many times before, expecting things to be the same—but they are not. You might be understandably stressed out or anxious because of the unfamiliar setting. Things have been moved, a wall or a room that used to exist is gone or a wall stands where none had previously been. Laborers or other workers coming and going added to the increased energy levels involved in a renovation or restoration project, and this may be enough to provide the spiritual or psychic energy needed for a spirit to begin manifesting.

Ghosts can get angry at the noisy intrusions onto their territory. Workers clumping about and using power tools or other equipment day in and day out would be unnerving to most living beings, and so it may be with a spirit. It is common for a spirit to form an attachment to a house or building, especially if they were the former owners or many memories are connected to the dwelling. Ghosts can become distraught over any changes or intrusions, especially if they are major. They feel they own the property or are the caretakers. They may also have the sense that they are still alive. Thus, when someone comes in and tries to make changes without their permission, it upsets them. The ghost might begin sabotaging or hindering the work. Occasionally, spirits form attachments that take on a more malignant form of paranormal activity. The current dwellers may begin having nightmares, objects may be thrown at them, mysterious scratches or bruises may show up on their bodies while they are sleeping, among other unsettling measures. This is all meant to scare the inhabitants and stop the construction or renovation. It is also possible that a ghost is jealous or spiteful of the changes being made. People encountering problems while renovating or restoring a home might do well to attempt to communicate with the spirit in order to appease them.

THE NIMS NEIGHBORHOOD OF Muskegon is bordered by Lakeshore Drive, Western Avenue, Laketon Avenue and Beidler Street. The homes in this neighborhood are for the most part of average size and price. There are a few older homes that are considered historic, including a one-hundred-year-old home that was recently moved from the Nims School lot to the downtown area. There are several historic buildings in the area. These include Lakeshore House and the Hume House. The backbone of the neighborhood historically is the former Nims School, named for lumber baron Frederick Nims. He was born in Clinton, Michigan, in 1839. He was a successful lawyer and sawmill owner as well as a friend and advisor to Charles Hackley. While serving in the Muskegon Improvement Company, he was influential in coordinating charitable organizations. In addition, he was a trustee for the Hackley fund and active in the planning and construction of Hackley Hospital. One of the main streets in the Nims neighborhood, running east–west, is Southern Avenue. The neighborhood is a slightly aging one. Many of the homes were built sometime in the early 1930s or 1940s. A few are rumored to be haunted. One rumor involves a former boardinghouse that dates to around 1910. Whispers of strange occurrences have circulated for years. Former tenants told of hearing strange sounds and seeing shadowy figures, televisions turning on and off by themselves and doors opening and closing on their own. Children who had to pass by the building on their way home from school were warned not to even look at the place. In time, the reasons for this faded into local urban legend, as typical childhood rumors tend to go. The remnants of the story crop up from time to time, especially around Halloween, undoubtedly with a few embellishments.

This particular neighborhood ghost was encountered about ten years ago at a house located somewhere near Division Street. This was a two-story house with a basement and a detached one-stall garage. The entire property was bordered by a small fence. An east–west alley runs behind the house. The house is believed to have been built sometime before the 1930s. A preservation crew consisting of Tom, Bill and Nick arrived at the house around 7:00 a.m. one morning. They drove down the alley and parked behind the house. Their boss had arrived earlier and was already in the house taking "before" photos. The three crew members waited in their truck. As they sat and waited for their boss to finish, Tom looked toward the house. He was a little surprised to see a man standing at the back door, behind the storm door. He could tell that the man was tall and thin but couldn't make out any other features. No one was in the house except his boss, but he could tell that this wasn't his boss. He pointed the man out to the other two and asked, "Who's that guy standing by the door?" One of them replied that it was probably a neighbor trying to see what was going on. Tom felt that was an odd answer, as a neighbor wouldn't be in the house. He was quite sure they were not talking about the same man. But he knew what he saw: a strange man standing in the doorway. Still puzzled but not wishing to make a big deal of it, Tom just said, "Oh, ok" and let the subject drop. After their boss had finished taking his photos, the crew went into the house. It was completely trashed. There were holes in the walls where the plaster had fallen off the narrow strips of boards used to finish interior walls. Plaster littered the floor. The former tenant had ripped out most of the copper wires from the walls, likely to sell as scrap metal. The men immediately set to work cleaning up the mess and clearing the house.

Tom spent most of the morning on the main floor, in the room where the back door was located and where he had first seen the tall, thin man. Tom was surprised to see that he was still there. As Tom worked, he occasionally caught a glimpse of him out of the corner of his eye, watching him work. Although Tom was aware this might be an apparition or a ghost watching him, he didn't say anything to Bill and Nick. But it wasn't long before the others became suspicious that they had company of the paranormal kind. Around 10:00 a.m., Bill went over to Tom and said, a little apprehensively, "Hey, about that guy you talking about earlier?" Tom asked, "You mean the tall, skinny guy by the back door?" Bill replied, "Yeah." Tom knew right then that he was not the only one who was being watched by this thin, quiet spirit. The three men continued clearing the main floor that morning. They picked up and bagged trash, took everything off the walls, tore down the curtains and blinds and removed shelves. Basically, anything that was not part of the structure had to go. They were good at their job; when they were done, not a single nail was left in the walls. By this time, they had filled the dumpster, so Bill and Nick left to take it to the dump. Tom was left alone in the house. He decided to work on clearing the basement and went downstairs. It was musty, dark and a little creepy, but not the kind of basement one sees in horror movies, when someone is warned, "Don't go down in the basement."

The house had an older furnace with vents that sprawled out throughout the basement and up through the floor into the house. It resembled a huge aluminum spider or octopus. Having worked on many older homes, Tom was familiar with these types of basements, so he didn't feel uneasy. He got to work moving boxes around, putting trash into bags and taking it all up the steps. The basement steps happened to be near the back door where he had seen the apparition. There was nothing on the stairs, but he tripped several times while carrying some of the heavier items. Tom thought this was a little weird, as he wasn't the clumsy sort. He continued to trip each time he went up the stairs. After a few minutes of this, he began to get a little frustrated. Then he tripped again, this time falling. He got a little angry. He decided to blame all this tripping and falling on the "man." By that point, Tom felt certain that this "man" was a ghost. He yelled out at him, "Come on, are you kidding me?," or something to that effect.

Still miffed at being tripped up, Tom proceeded to go up the stairs to the living room. He was going to have a talk with this man or ghost or whatever it was. Speaking out loud to the house and, hopefully, the ghost, Tom explained that he did not make this mess in "his" house. He was there to clean it and make it look better. As they headed back to their truck at the end of the day, Tom and Bill saw the man again, but neither worker mentioned it to Nick. When they all got back to the truck, Tom and Bill began talking about what happened, trying to process what they had seen. They tried to keep the conversation light, but they both knew this was out of the ordinary. After listening to their conversation for a few minutes, Nick spoke up. He told them that while he was working in the basement, the man was walking back and forth outside the window, in the fenced-in yard. Still trying to be nonchalant and find a reasonable explanation for the incident, Tom suggested it may have been someone from the gas company who was there to shut the gas off. That seemed to be a reasonable explanation. But when they came back the next day, the gas was still on.

Tom felt that his work went a little easier after his conversation with the ghost; no more inexplicable tripping incidents. The energy level in the house seemed to ease up a bit. Bill and Nick came back after dumping the trailer. Bill went upstairs to work on the second floor, which was also a big mess. Nick picked up where Tom had left off in the basement. Tom stayed on the main floor, working on some repairs that required him to take his gloves off. Sometime that afternoon, he needed to put them back on, but he couldn't find them. They were gone. He spent upward of an hour searching for his gloves, without luck. He reasoned that they should be easy to spot. They were bright yellow. The main floor was completely empty. He continued searching for another half hour and was about to give up when Bill came downstairs to get his water bottle, which was sitting on the kitchen counter. That was the only remaining surface where they could have placed anything, and there was nothing else in sight. Tom's gloves were not there, either. Nick came up from the basement at the same time. Nick yelled at Tom and pointed to something in the middle of the kitchen floor. Tom turned and looked. There were his gloves. Tom said, "Good one." They all had a good laugh at this. They knew how the gloves got there. Tom got pranked by the ghost again.

Tom and Bill went back to the house several days later. Nick was not with them this time. It was still early, not yet 7:00 a.m. It was a warm, sunny day. They decided to take a short nap in the truck before starting work. They had been asleep for about ten minutes when a loud, metallic bang coming from the truck woke them. It sounded as though someone had thrown a baseball bat into the bed of the truck. Not knowing what was going on, one of them grabbed a pipe or a tire iron and jumped out of the truck. They looked around. No one was in sight. Tom looked at Bill and said jokingly, "Well, I think he is telling us it's time to go to work." Their nap over, they went in and got to work. This was the last day of preservation, so there wasn't much left to do. While Tom scrubbed the bathroom on the main floor near the back door, Bill finished up some work on the upstairs rooms. Tom was pleased that the ghost was not there watching him. He felt that the energy in the house was different and actually quite pleasant compared to last time. When Bill came down to grab something, Tom told him, "Hey, he's not watching me today." Bill laughed and said that was because the ghost was now watching him. Thinking that Bill was joking, Tom laughed. When they were done working, Tom asked him what he had meant. Bill told him the ghost had been peering at him all morning from behind the walls, through the holes in lath and plaster.

The men completed their preservation work in record time. They were always efficient, but this was not a house they wanted to hang around in. On the last day, they went from room to room, double-checking to make sure they had gotten it all. Tom looked around to make sure the main room was completely cleared. Everything had been, swept, cleared and cleaned. It was spotless. Anything that wasn't nailed down had been removed. As he walked by a shelf, something caught Tom's eye. In the middle of the shelf, which had been completely empty, was a 1973 half dollar. Tom chuckled and put the coin in his pocket. Their ghostly supervisor had approved of their work. He had even left them a bonus.

5

UNLUCKY HORSESHOE AND OTHER BAD OMENS

GHOST OF THE CHRISTMAS TREE SHIP

E veryone wants to have good luck. It's the idea behind carrying a rabbit's foot, finding a four-leaf clover or nailing a horseshoe over your doorway. The problem is that good luck can go bad in a hurry if things get turned upside down—like an upside-down horseshoe. When that horseshoe is on a ship, it is an even worse omen, according to sailor lore. Legend has it that an upside-down horseshoe, along with other bad omens, was responsible for the mysterious disappearance of the *Rouse-Simmons*, whose ghostly apparition is now doomed to haunt the Great Lakes' shores. Ships that mysteriously vanish or appear out of the mists centuries after they disappeared have entertained and intrigued us for hundreds of years. Any vessel found with no living crew on board is considered a phantom ship. A ghost ship can be a ghostly apparition or a ship found adrift without its crew, such as the *Flying Dutchman* or the *Mary Celeste*, which was found inexplicably floating adrift without its crew. When we think of ghost ships, we typically picture vessels found on the high seas. However, the oceans are not their only haunts. Ghost ships are said to travel over smaller bodies of water as well. In fact, the Great Lakes have had more than their share of disappearances, wreckages and ghost ships. More than six thousand ships are known to have disappeared or been wrecked under mysterious circumstances in the Great Lakes over the span of maritime history. Among these are the *Le Griffon* in the seventeenth century, the *Rosabell*, the *Carl A. Bradley*, the *Lady Elgin* and, more recently, the *Edmund Fitzgerald*. Many ships have succumbed to the unpredictable nature of Lake Michigan. It has a penchant for whipping up storms at a moment's notice. Conventional wisdom attributes these occurrences to the weather. Others believe there is something more mysterious behind these incidents, something more than bad omens and horseshoes but a little more scientific. Some researchers believe that many shipwrecks and disappearances are caused by an area known as the Michigan Triangle. This region has seen more unexplained disappearances than the famed Bermuda Triangle. In recent years, more than forty planes have inexplicably gone missing or crashed.

While not as well as known as the Bermuda Triangle, this anomalous area is said to inexplicably take ships down into its depths, never to be seen again. The triangle goes across Lake Michigan from Manitowoc, Wisconsin, east to Ludington, Michigan, then south to Benton Harbor, Michigan.

One of the disappearances involved one of Charles Hackley's lumber schooners, the *Rouse-Simmons*, which was affectionately dubbed the "Christmas Tree Ship." In addition to being a beloved icon throughout the Lake Michigan region, it has joined the long list of ships that have succumbed to its murky depths. Through legends and reported sightings over the years since it disappeared, the Christmas Tree Ship has become a maritime ghost of Christmas past. During Christmas holidays, it was common for Great Lakes lumber-hauling ships to carry Christmas trees to sell from their decks, the *Rouse-Simmons* among them. The *Rouse-Simmons* was a wood schooner built in 1868 by Allan, McClelland & Company in Milwaukee, Wisconsin. It was large, with a length of 125 feet, three masts and a five-hundred-ton cargo capacity. It was commissioned by Wisconsin businessman Rouse Simmons at a cost of $14,000. Built specifically to transport lumber across the Great Lakes, it was eventually purchased by lumber baron Charles Hackley in 1873. Hackley's lumber operations stretched along the Lake Michigan ports. Hackley used the ship until 1893. He sold it to Captain August Schuenemann in 1906.

The *Rouse-Simmons* made runs from Grand Haven to Chicago on a regular basis and to the various markets around the lake for almost twenty years, but it began to show its age. In addition, the ship had already sunk and was raised once. August Schuenemann began his traditional Christmas tree voyages sometime in the late 1800s, making annual runs to Chicago and other ports after loading up with trees from Manistique, Michigan. Before arriving in port, the ship's crew would decorate a tree and tie it to one of the masts. When electric lights came into use, these were added, making the festive ship quite a sight to behold. Captain August Schuenemann lost his life on one such Christmas tree voyage, although on a different ship. The *Rouse-Simmons's* cherished holiday pilgrimages were then carried on by his brother Herman, who, with Captain Charles Nelson and three others, purchased the ship. He was a shrewd businessman, but Schuenemann would give trees out to those who could not afford to buy one. Trees were a luxury and sometimes not easy to come by in states where little forestland could be found. Thus his arrivals at ports throughout the region were greeted with joy, especially by children. Herman became a well-known figure throughout the Great Lakes region, and it wasn't long before he began to be known as "Captain Santa."

Unfortunately for Captain Santa and his crew, unexpected tragedy struck one November day. Seafaring stories attribute the ship's certain doom to bad luck brought on by a hanging horseshoe and the presence of thirteen crew members. Others speculate that the vessel was the victim of the Michigan Triangle's mysterious energies. Others attribute the tragedy to the Great Lakes' unpredictable weather patterns. Understandably, the lakes can be quite volatile, especially in winter months, making late-season trips dangerous. Seasonal storms can come out of nowhere. Lake Michigan is known to be the site of sudden storms and squalls. Lake temperatures in the winter are at or below freezing, often making travel treacherous. The Great Lakes is the largest group of freshwater lakes in the world, with a total area of 94,250 square miles. Lake Michigan is the second largest of the lakes at 22,404 square miles. It is the only one of the group completely within the United States. At about 300 miles in length, 120 miles across and 300 feet deep, Lake Michigan is more akin to a small ocean than a lake. It is bordered by the states of Michigan, Wisconsin, Illinois and Indiana. Major ports along the lake include Milwaukee and Green Bay, Wisconsin; Chicago, Illinois; Gary, Indiana; and Muskegon, Michigan. While the term *lake* may define these bodies of water as meek and mild, they are anything but docile. Many people have been fooled by their appearances. Their vast expanses of open water, rogue waves and unpredictable weather conditions make them as treacherous and dangerous as any of the world's oceans, perhaps even more so. The Great Lakes are known to be unforgiving. In the late fall and winter months, a sunny, clear day can turn into a full-blown blizzard in a matter of minutes. The most ferocious of these storms is known by area sailors as the "Witch of November."

On November 21, 1912, Captain Santa set out for Chicago on his annual holiday after taking on a load of Christmas trees in Thompson, Michigan. Captain Nelson had warned Schuenemann to cancel the trip, to no avail. Herman didn't want to be iced in at the harbor. So, despite the pleadings

Lighthouse at Pere Marquette Channel.

of their families, advice from a well-seasoned captain, the apprehensions of the crew and the knowledge that a storm was imminent, they embarked on a ship that was almost fifty years old. The ship left port with a reduced crew, as three of the men refused to board. The usual sixteen-man crew was now down to thirteen—a bad omen. At the start, sailing conditions were good. In spite of the Great Lakes' well-known proclivity for whipping up brutal storms in the winter months at a moment's notice and warnings of the Witch of November, Lake Michigan had been surprisingly quiet that year. Accompanying Captain Schuenemann on this portentous voyage were the second in command, Captain Charles Nelson, and thirteen crew members. By other accounts, there was a crew of sixteen. The *Rouse-Simmons* was loaded with between four thousand and five thousand trees. The trees were bundled and stacked several feet high on the deck as well as in the

Barge at Muskegon port.

Craft boat coming into Muskegon Channel.

cargo hold. This made the ship extremely heavy, and it sat dangerously low in the water, increasing the possibility that water would overtake the deck in a storm. The age-worn vessel was overloaded. Three crew members refused to go aboard, even forfeiting their pay. They were fearful that the aging and unstable schooner, overloaded and with a storm coming, would capsize. Their worst fears came to pass. A full-blown blizzard quickly developed. When the ship set sail, a light fog blanketed the lake. A winter squall developed quickly, and it wasn't long before gale-force winds began buffeting the old ship as it neared the Wisconsin border. The temperature dropped from forty degrees to below freezing. The icy downpour pelted the ship with heavy, wet snow and ice, swiftly covering the ship's rigging, sails and the thousands of Christmas trees, creating a treacherous situation. Freezing waves washed over the sides, quickly covering everything with an arctic blanket of ice, including the trees on deck. The already-heavy load became even heavier. Sometime over the next two days, the ship was battered by gale-force winds and frigid waves, which continued to wash over the sides. Two crewmen were swept overboard, possibly while trying to secure the trees or steady the ship. The ship had only one lifeboat, and it was certainly not big enough to hold all of the men, even if they had time to climb aboard.

The *Rouse-Simmons* was last seen around 3:00 p.m. on November 23, 1912. Its flag was flying at half-mast, indicating that the ship was in trouble. This distress signal was seen by members of a rescue station on the Wisconsin shoreline, and a team was hastily dispatched. Regrettably, they were unable to reach the vessel, getting only about eight miles from the ship's last known location. Another team south of where the ship was last spotted, near Two Rivers, Wisconsin, was sent out. They were also unable to locate the ship. A few days later, men fishing with nets found treetops tangled in their nets near the ship's last known location. When the Christmas tree ship did not arrive in Chicago as scheduled, Schuenemann's family became concerned. Another search team was sent out, without success. It wasn't long before hundreds of Christmas trees began washing up on shore. This was a sure sign that something bad had befallen the ship. For many months after, Christmas trees were seen floating to shore. A bottle was found washed ashore. It included a message from the captain: "Everybody, goodbye. I guess we are thru. Leaking badly. God help us. Signed: Herman Schuenemann." Another message in a bottle was found, stating: "Friday…everybody goodbye. I guess we are all through. During the night the small boat washed overboard. Leaking bad. Invald and Steve lost too. God help us." On December 14, a Coast Guard cutter set out from Chicago to search for the ship and its crew. The search was called off after no sign of the ship or the men was found.

The *Rouse-Simmons* was officially recorded as being lost due to a sudden winter storm, but several curious aspects have added to the mystery. A survey of the shipwreck was performed in 2006 by the Wisconsin Historical Society. While it is commonly thought that a sudden winter storm doomed the vessel, an interview with Captain George E. Sogge about a month after the incident seems to contradict this. Sogge said that visibility to the Kewaunee station was clear when the distress signal went out. Furthermore, no storm was being reported at the time that the ship was last seen at 3:00 p.m. While it had started to snow when the rescue ship went out to search, the skies were clear when the distress signal was sent. Also curious is the fact that, despite the ship being apparently close to the Wisconsin shoreline when it began to flounder, the men decided to stay with the ship instead of attempting to swim for it. It is speculated that the icy temperature of the water and the hundreds of Christmas trees floating in the water were deterrents, keeping the men on the ship. The trees bumping together in the water posed a grave danger to any swimmers. Furthermore, the strong undertow of the lake, churned up by the storm, would have no doubt pulled men beneath the frigid waves. As a result, the crew members may have felt it safer to stay with the ship and hope for the best. All in all, it was a combination that proved disaster for the thirteen men and Captains Nelson and Schuenemann. None survived that fateful day in 1912. It is said that the Great Lakes never gives up their dead. Lake Michigan was true to its word that day. It held the captains and crew tight in its icy grip at the bottom of the lake. Their remains were never found.

The final resting place of the Christmas tree ship was found in 180 feet of water by divers in 1971, close to where it was last seen near Two Rivers, Wisconsin. The remains of Christmas trees still clung to the vessel. Captain Schuenemann's intact wallet washed up several years later. Archaeologists studying the wreckage noted that the ship's anchor was down, an indication of a possible last-ditch effort to keep the ship afloat. It is theorized that the vessel was overcome by large waves, sinking it to the bottom. There is speculation that Captain Santa, in trying to maximize his profits, had created a dangerous situation by ignoring the warnings, being fully aware of how changeable the lake could be at that time of year. Investigators also found the *Rouse-Simmons* to be structurally unable to withstand a storm such as the one that occurred on that fateful day, especially in light of its overloaded state and age. In October 1905, the already age-worn schooner was making a run when one of its masts was blown down in a sudden storm, making the ship unstable. The ship's cook, convinced that the crew would soon perish, penned a note to his wife and placed it in a bottle in hopes that someone would find it and give it to her. It eventually washed up on to the Ludington shore. Luckily, the *Rouse-Simmons* was rescued that time.

So, what doomed the *Rouse-Simmons*? Was it a typical Lake Michigan storm, or did the disregard of many omens seal its fate? First it was the rats. It is a well-known sailing superstition that rats will leave a ship that is destined to sink. So when some of the sailors saw rats leaving the *Rouse-Simmons*, they felt certain it was doomed. Perhaps it is rats' cunning and keen instincts that account for their fleeing a doomed craft. This attribute may not be appreciated, given their apparent lack of empathy in leaving the crew behind. It certainly does not endear them to sailors. More likely, the crew members started looking for other omens or portents, as sailors tend to be a superstitious lot. They were not disappointed.

Next it was the three crewmen who refused to make the trip, leaving thirteen, a number known to foreshadow bad luck. Then there were the premonitions made by Captain Nelson's daughter. In spite of his daughter's pleadings and misgivings, the captain was determined to honor the commitment. Alfida reportedly begged her father not to go, citing her premonition that the ship would suffer a disaster. He promised her that it would be his final tree run. Schuenemann also made this same promise to his wife and daughters. Tragically, Alfida was right. Had Captain Nelson taken his daughter's premonition seriously and insisted that the voyage be canceled, the calamity could have been avoided.

There have been many stories of people having premonitions of tragedies, such as train wrecks or plane crashes that led them to cancel trips or otherwise miss a voyage or flight. While skeptics attribute this to mere chance or coincidence, when a premonition can be documented before an event happens, it gives credence to something inexplicable occurring. Premonitions come in many forms, from an overpowering "gut" feeling that something is going to happen, to a disturbing dream that seems more real than usual. They can even take the form of powerful, real-time visions, in which one is watching a future event play out in front of them, as if on a movie screen. Such visions are often not specific, just unexplained feelings of sadness or anxiety that something has happened or is about to happen. One does not have to be considered psychic or sensitive to have a premonition. When something dire could happen to a family member, a premonition might occur due to the powerful bonds that exist between close relatives or loved ones.

The next omen for the crew of the *Rouse-Simmons* struck when the wind knocked their good-luck horseshoe loose so that it was hanging sideways instead of upward. Horseshoes are typically nailed above a door or to the mast of a ship with the open ends up. It is believed that this keeps the good luck in and has the power to turn away a storm. Horseshoes have been used as a good luck charm and a protective symbol for years, protecting against evil and bringing good fortune. Their power comes from their being made from iron, a metal long known for strength and for the ability to withstand fire. Its power may also lie in its shape: a curved bow. It was also considered unlucky to change the name of a ship, and while its name wasn't officially changed, the *Rouse-Simmons* began to be known as the "Christmas tree ship." To top it off, it was Friday when the ship set sail. No sailor worth his salt would set sail on a Friday. They would even wait until one minute after midnight to set sail in order to avoid this bad omen.

Although the ship and everyone aboard were lost to the lake, leaving only legends, the Christmas tree tradition lived on for some time. Herman Schuenemann's wife and two daughters continued his holiday tradition and sold trees from the docks until the Great Depression, when the business closed in 1933. Even now, the Chicago-based Coast Guard cutter *Mackinac* delivers Christmas trees to people in need in honor of Captain Santa and his cherished tradition and to commemorate the day the cutter went out to search for survivors. The story of the Christmas tree ship and its tragic end has become an integral part of the shared history of Michigan, Illinois and Wisconsin. Herman's widow died in 1933 and was buried in Arcadia Park Cemetery in Chicago. On her tomb is a single evergreen tree. People who visit the grave site are said to be met by the overpowering scent of pine, although no such trees are nearby.

It has been over one hundred years since that fateful November day, but the *Rouse-Simmons* is still said to sail across the lake, often in times of inclement weather, to warn others to stay off the lakes. It can be seen drifting through the fog, a lighted festive Christmas tree sitting atop its mast. It glides along the coastline guided by the ghostly crew desperately trying to make their way through the storm. The ship is also said to appear several days before Christmas, its solemn voyage a murky fragment of a Christmas lost. Believers and the curious will often stand along the shore to catch a glimpse of it. Some claim to have witnessed it gliding silently through the mists along the Lake Michigan shoreline—its sails ripped and tattered and flapping about as if buffeted by the wind. A lone ghostly sailor is said to stand on the bow, waving a lit lantern back and forth, desperately trying to get someone's attention to their plight, unaware that he is no longer among the living, as if in penance. Were the omens and portents a warning that could have been avoided, or was the ship doomed from the start? Consequently, if omens and portents are indeed warnings, then those who ignore them do so at their own peril. This was a lesson lost for the captain and crew of the Christmas tree ship.

6

A Treat for Ella Amelia

Pastry Shop Ghosts

Alone figure stands thoughtfully looking down at the rows of delicacies in the pastry shop. There are so many to choose from. After a moment, the figure drifts away without choosing anything. The shopkeeper is oblivious to any of this. Other than feeling an odd coldness near the counter, she is unaware that anyone is there. This is probably a good thing, because if she had seen the figure, she would have quickly realized it was no ordinary shopper. It was a ghost, one of two said to haunt the building. One might be that of Ella Amelia, a ghost with a sweet tooth.

It has long been the case that mysterious things happen from time to time at the building at 1925 Lakeshore. This building is situated in the community of Lakeside, one of Muskegon's early settlements. In addition to the growth that the influx of industries brought to Muskegon, its growth was also aided by the inclusion of small, independent communities that lay along the southern shore of Muskegon Lake. A number of these communities thrived and became townships in their own right, standing alongside the city even today. Others, like Bluffton, "Pinchtown" and Port Sherman, were absorbed into the city of Muskegon. Lakeside was another one of these communities. The community began in 1870 as a small settlement near the lumber mills with shanties and small houses. These simple houses were built for the men who worked at the mills. The community comprised little except for a post office. Later, small shops and businesses began cropping up. The village had what was known as a "curiosity shop," owned by a Mr. and Mrs. Burge. Customers were greeted by the gentle tinkle of a small bell above the door. In addition to the usual groceries and sundries, Burge's had an assortment of curiosities and souvenirs filling one end of their entire living room. Shoppers and their children spent much time in fascination browsing these interesting sights.

In contrast to the overall simplicity of this rural area, in the late 1800s, the area was one of the wealthiest. The region between Bluffton and Lakeside was still woodlands, with a dirt road winding along the lake near the dunes. This road connected the communities of Port Sherman, Bluffton and Lakeside. Bluffton, originally known as Millville, eventually became home to an actor's colony. Buster Keaton, one of the world's most beloved silent-screen stars, made frequent visits to the area and his family's summer home. Port Sherman, or Laketon, began as an Ottawa tribal village with four hundred to five hundred inhabitants at one point. Later, several sawmills were built by Smith, Fowler and Company on the site. Sherman House, a vacation resort, was erected in 1874, and it became a favorite spot for Chicago-area vacationers. These three villages formed Lakeside Township in 1875. They were incorporated in 1883. Squeezed between Muskegon and Lakeside was the settlement known as "Pinchtown." The nickname derived from the town's being a narrow strip of land that belonged to neither village. This odd zoning detail was swiftly taken advantage of by Jim Robinson, who built a saloon, Lakeshore House, on the site. The police had no jurisdiction over the goings-on in Pinchtown. With no closing time or other laws to rein things in, Lakeshore House quickly became the place to go for boxing matches, cockfights, all-night card games and gambling.

As is common in many cities, many of Muskegon's streets are named for their prominent citizens, some of whom were lumber barons. Some of Lakeside's prominent citizens who had streets named for them include Seth D. Estes, Newcomb McGraft, George Tillotson, P. Misner and J.W. Moon. McGraft Park was named for Newcomb McGraft and connects the Glenside neighborhood to the Lakeside district. McGraft came to Muskegon around 1870, along with his employer, an uncle of President Grover Cleveland. McGraft partnered with A.S. Montgomery, who was influential in the building of the Grand Rapids and Indiana Railroad Company. McGraft also owned a lumber company and operated a sawmill. As an industrialist with a vested interest in Muskegon, McGraft was a firm believer in a prosperous future for the growing city. Ruddimen Street

Building at 1924 Lakeshore Drive. It is the location of various small businesses and shops, with apartments upstairs.

and Ruddimen Creek are named for two brothers, George and John. The brothers built a mill at the mouth of what is now Ruddiman Creek. John built a steam mill in North Muskegon and a flour mill in Bear Lake. George also opened a lumber mill in North Muskegon. George lived on Lake Street, which later became Lakeshore Drive. With a population of around 1,700 in 1883, Lakeside became incorporated into a village, becoming part of the city of Muskegon in 1888. Many of the men with businesses located in Lakeside were also founding fathers and had large homes downtown.

Before the street was renamed Lakeshore Drive, the building's address was listed as Lake Street. There has been a succession of tenants living at the address over the years, including Clarence Chase, superintendent of the Chase Piano Company. The Chase Piano Company manufactured high-quality pianos in Muskegon for many years, turning out upward of fifty a year. Chase pianos drew praise from around the world and were said to be some of the best in the country at the time, making Clarence Chase quite well off. In 1926, a shoe repair shop operated by Edgar E. Colburn and Oscar D. Robinson was located in the building.

Early records state that in 1921, thirty-year-old Ella Amelia Johnson had also lived at that address. Not much is known about her life, other than that she died of tuberculosis. However, a few things can be surmised by the social conditions of the day. It's possible that she was single and lived alone, which was not common but not unheard of. Women in the 1920s were less reserved than their Victorian sisters, rejecting domesticity and pursuing roles in the public domain. This trend began in the late 1890s, ostensibly with the iconic symbol of the "Gibson Girl." Women began shedding the restrictive corsets, heavy petticoats and frilly dresses. They began to enjoy greater freedoms, playing sports like tennis and riding bicycles. The emergence of the new woman had begun, challenging gender and strict social norms. They began voicing their need for autonomy and independence. Women were beginning to embrace a new confidence and capabilities, and it would be nice to think of Ella as an independent young lady. Following the era of the Gibson Girl, the "flapper" came into vogue. The flapper became synonymous with excess, frivolity and flaunting the restrictions of the past. But not all women espoused this iconic image. Changing demographics also contributed to the rise of the independent woman. Many were single and earned a living on their own but were still subject to social norms, which tended to focus on domestic life. Some women still lived lives of drudgery, working as domestics or servants, even though times were changing. While they found jobs in the public domain, they continued to be at a disadvantage politically and economically. Many worked in mills or factories. If Ella was single and lived close to local factories, especially the piano factory, it is reasonable to think that she was employed at one of them. Unfortunately, tuberculosis was becoming widespread in the United States in the early 1900s, along with smallpox, yellow fever, cholera, typhoid fever and typhus. Muskegon, like many other towns its size, struggled to address the contagion issue. TB is a lingering disease. Ella may have suffered for quite some time before passing away, alone in her apartment. The building is now home to a number of small, independent businesses with apartments upstairs. Some unusual events were said to have happened at a pastry shop formerly located there. A number of people have also reported sensing an unseen presence in the shop. They have never felt anything foreboding or frightening, just the presence itself.

An investigation was conducted by Candi Hess and her husband, Rick, after reaching out to the shop owner. After a security camera showed the shop's Christmas tree falling or being pushed, the owners felt it couldn't have fallen over on its own. The lower floor of the building is divided into

Chase Piano Company. *Muskegon Picture Collection. Hackley Public Library. Local History & Genealogy Department, Muskegon, Michigan.*

An SLS camera reportedly picked up the image of a ghost standing near the pastry shop counter during a paranormal investigation. This is a fictionalized representation of that event. *Illustration by ©Gabe Schillman, www.studio37arts.com, 2022, Newaygo, Michigan.*

two shops, side by side. As an empath, Candi felt there was definitely a lot of paranormal energy in the shop and sensed the energy of two spirits. While the upstairs was not investigated, Candi said she could feel the energy from the stairs. The spirit energy was not believed to be malevolent—they just wanted someone to know they were there. A spirit box was then employed. When the spirits were asked if they were the ones who had knocked over the Christmas tree, the answer was "yes." Jealousy could have been a factor, or it may have been the pranking nature of ghosts. The investigators were also able to obtain activity on EVP as well as on a SLS camera. The camera purportedly shows a spirit near the counter. It isn't known who these spirits were in life. One could very well be Ella Amelia. Candi explained that once the spirit passes into the spirit world, they lose the connection to who they were in life. The pastry shop is no longer there, and it is not known if anyone else has experienced spirit energy since. Ghosts are known to become attached to either a building or objects within a building. If a spirit had to be stuck anywhere, a pastry shop might be the best place to spend some time. After all, who can resist the aroma of fresh pastry straight from the oven? Apparently, not even a ghost.

7

ON WITH THE SHOW

FRAUENTHAL THEATER
AND THE GHOST OF P.J.

The audience claps as the curtains rise. Lights pan over the stage. Behind the curtain, an elegant man dressed in a top hat, black tux and stylish white scarf draped confidently around his neck peers out at the crowd. Satisfied that there is a full house, he then moves swiftly along the aisle seats. Seeing that everything appears to be in order, he disappears. Having everything go well on opening night is important, and every theater owner wants the show to be spectacular. Unfortunately for this owner, if it was a flop, he couldn't fire anyone, although perhaps he could haunt them. Meet "P.J.," one of Muskegon's most sophisticated and intriguing ghosts, believed by some to be the spirit of Paul Schlossman. P.J. is a well-dressed apparition said to haunt the Frauenthal Theater. The theater, originally the Michigan Theater, was built in 1929 by Paul Schlossman at a cost of almost $700,000 in the heart of the business district. This magnificent 1930s movie palace on Western and Third in Muskegon was one of three built by the Schlossman Company and designed by architect C. Howard Crane. They also built the Rialto, the Majestic and the Regent. Later, after being appointed secretary-treasurer of the Strand Amusement Company, he had the Strand Theater constructed in Muskegon Heights. Schlossman paid a great deal of attention to the construction of the Michigan and worked closely with Crane on every aspect. He wanted a theater that showed "talkies." When the Michigan opened in 1930, it was praised for its beauty and elegance. It seemed that Schlossman had brought the glamor of Hollywood to Muskegon. Opening night was an immense

Frauenthal Theater. *Illustration by ©Gabe Schillman, www.studio37arts.com, 2022, Newaygo, Michigan.*

success, and newspaper articles boasted that Muskegon now had the best theater in the state. The Michigan Theater was built in the Moorish, or Spanish Renaissance, architectural style, with its characteristic opulent themes. Gold accents draped every corner, and whimsical cherubs, as well as imposing griffins, stood guard over the façades. Ornate chandeliers and light fixtures decorated the ceilings and walls. Comfortable chairs were vibrantly colored and featured lush velour, as were the intricately patterned Moorish-style carpets. The ceiling was elaborately embellished with shells. The walls had lavishly patterned terra-cotta plasterwork, cornered arches and ornamental carvings. An immense stage was enclosed with luxuriant, bright-red drapes. High above the seats on the main floor was the oculus, or centerpiece.

Sometime in the 1950s, after being active for over thirty years, the Michigan Theater was closed for renovations. In keeping with the fashion of the day, which opted for modern and sleek styles, the gold and colorful

Left: Frauenthal Theater with *Muskegon, Together Rising* sculpture in foreground symbolizing the rebirth of downtown. *Sculpture by Richard Hunt, 2019.*

Below: Stage at Frauenthal Theater. The ghost of "P.J." is said to peek at theatergoers and staff from behind stage curtains. *Photo courtesy of Derek Wong MI, 2021. https://derekwongmi.com.*

Moorish features were painted a subdued shade of beige. When it reopened, it served as a movie theater for a time. Schlossman's company was dissolved, and the theater began a slow descent into decline. It was closed and boarded up by the 1970s. In its deteriorated state, it was due to be torn down, but a citizens' group began efforts to save the aging theater. The group was assisted by both local and county officials and the Community Foundation for Muskegon County. With an additional $1.5 million donation from A. Harold Frauenthal, an earnest effort to save Muskegon's golden-age icon began. Frauenthal purchased the theater block, intending to offer symphony or musical performances, as well as movies and other events. A master plan for renovation by the Community Foundation was proposed, with a bond issue approved by Muskegon County residents. Restoration work began in 1998. The theater was restored to its prior beauty and opulence, with the addition of state-of-the-art sound system and lighting and stage riggings. The lobby now connects the old theater with the Hilt Building. While Paul Schlossman may not be remembered, the building remains as a magnificent testimony to the grandeur of Muskegon in the 1930s and his vision for it.

Paul J. Schlossman was born on January 9, 1878, in Chicago. He spent almost twenty years as a traveling garment salesman before organizing the Square Clothing Company in 1911. With his business acumen and enterprising spirit, he soon made Square an immensely profitable business. But the garment industry wasn't the only place he would make his mark in the area. He owned large portions of some of the most profitable real estate in Muskegon. With his building of movie houses, he soon dominated the area's entertainment field. Paul's unique style stands out as being the very essence of what a showman should be. He is best remembered for his camel-hair coat, top hat tipped jauntily down over one eye and snow-white scarf wrapped around his neck. Paul could always be seen walking purposefully around the theater, making sure that everything was running smoothly. Perhaps this is why some think that it is none other than Schlossman's ghost that is still supervising what goes on at the theater, wearing his signature formal evening wear as he follows staff members or visitors around. The spirit is said to have appeared in the office and backstage, as well as in his former office.

One story comes down from a former staff member whose job it was to walk around to make sure all of the doors were secured. During nightly rounds, it was noted that seats would go down, as if someone had been sitting there. The ropes used to cordon off aisles would inexplicably fall off their stanchions. One night while going to the projection room, the worker

Buster Keaton statue. It was brought from Hollywood and placed in front of Frauenthal Theater in 2010 to symbolize Muskegon's own Hollywood star. *Sculpture by Emmanuel Snitkovsky.*

noted that the door would not budge. It was as if someone was pressing firmly against it. After a few moments of the worker trying, the door opened by itself. Frightened by this, the worker hurriedly finished up rounds and left. Some people have felt an oppressive or heavy sensation when entering the building. The halls seemed to have had a particularly eerie feel to them. There is one hall in particular where a few people apparently felt particularly uneasy upon entering. P.J. is also said to be seen peering at patrons from behind the stage curtain, as if looking to see how many people are in the audience, or perhaps wanting to make sure they had good seats. He would also walk the seat aisles, especially on the balcony. A paranormal investigation by West Michigan Paranormal Team in 2019 picked up some intriguing activity that possibly showed spirit manifestation. Much of the focus was placed on the office areas, where a presence or energy was said to have been felt. The team used EVP monitors as well as dowsing rods in several areas of the theater. While the team members were standing on the balcony talking, one of them reportedly received an EVP reading telling them to "hush." Although they did not pick up any visual manifestations or full-form apparitions, the team picked up a lot of activity on the balcony using a motion sensor. An orb was also photographed. In the office area, they were able to pick up a lot of communication energy, or "intelligent interactions," using a "Phasmobox."

Does the ghost of Paul Schlossman still walk the aisles and hallways of the Frauenthal Theater? We will probably never know for sure. Schlossman certainly loved it. He loved movies. He loved the glitz and the grandeur of it all. He might love that the glamour and grandness of this beloved palace has returned. Perhaps this is why he walks the halls of the theater, so that the magnificence of the movie theater's days will not be forgotten. As an avid showman and businessman, Schlossman took a keen interest in the day-to-day affairs of the theater, making sure all went as planned. This interest apparently has not waned, even though he has passed over the veil. Even now, Paul is believed to be on hand, wearing full theater attire, making sure everything is in tip-top order. As the saying goes, once a showman, always a showman. The show must go on, even in the afterlife.

8

I CAN SEE YOU

HAUNTED LANDS OF NORTHSHORE HOSPITAL

Shadows lurk in rooms, ice-cold air sweeps down hallways, ghostly orbs float over the land and discarnate voices are heard moaning and whispering. Welcome to Northshore Hospital. Enter if you dare. While the building was actually torn down years ago, this vacant lot on Holton Road in North Muskegon may be one of the city's most haunted locations. It is said to have been the scene of a range of strange encounters and unusual occurrences. The daring souls who once ventured into the dark and crumbling hospital described it as disturbing, evil and terrifying. If the stories can be believed, there is something paranormal going on there. Northshore Hospital was originally built as a tuberculosis sanatorium in 1926. At one time, tuberculosis (TB) was one of the most dreaded diseases known to mankind and the leading cause of death in America. Early scientists thought it was hereditary and could not be stopped, until Robert Koch discovered the TB bacteria in 1882. This discovery ushered in hopes for a cure, but it also brought fear. As a disproportionate number of the afflicted were centered in urban slums, where unsanitary conditions and overcrowding contributed to transmission, TB victims were frequently labeled as outcasts. In the late 1800s, Dr. Edward Trudeau promoted the idea of isolating tuberculosis patients, as he felt isolation sped recovery and that this would spare the healthy. Dr. Trudeau believed that exercise, fresh air, a healthy diet and rest were also vital to getting patients on the road to recovery. While this belief helped promote the use of sanatoriums and furthered research, it also helped continue the growing stigma associated with the illness. Muskegon's first doctor was Charles McSherry, MD. He came to the area in 1849 with his family. It wasn't long before Dr. McSherry and other physicians in the Muskegon area had to address the tuberculosis issue. The idea of a tuberculosis sanatorium began to gain momentum.

The dominant health concerns in Muskegon during that time were malaria, ague, diphtheria and lumbermill accidents. The prevention, treatment and isolation of these diseases and injuries were of utmost importance. As public health expanded in the 1900s, much emphasis was placed on improving sanitary conditions. The State Board of Health studied vital statistics, investigated the cause of diseases and advised on health matters. In the late 1800s, smallpox, yellow fever, cholera, typhoid fever and typhus were of concern in the United States. In 1878, U.S. Congress enacted laws in an effort to prevent the spread of contagious and infectious diseases. It was during that time that the Muskegon County Tuberculosis Association was established, along with a free clinic. Not long after, the association pressed forward with an aggressive campaign. Reformers used illustrative posters to propagandize and persuade in

Site of demolished Northshore Hospital. Holton, Michigan, 49444. *Map courtesy of Google Earth. http://www.earth.google.com.*

order to further their cause. At one time, over two thousand posters were distributed by public health officers. Christmas Seals was another method they used to promote and fund the idea. These methods proved effective in swaying public opinion, and construction on Northshore Hospital begun. After use of sanatoriums fell out of practice, the hospital was converted to use as a county mental facility. It was closed in 1979 after governmental funding for such projects dried up. The building sat abandoned for a number of years, sometimes being the go-to place for partying teenagers, derelicts and curiosity-seekers, before being torn down in 2004.

Although the building was demolished and the patients and staff are long gone, something is still there, something that seems to forbid people to come near it. Upon entering the building, visitors were met with graffiti-painted images of eyes, monsters or other bizarre creatures, as well as phrases like "House of the dead," "I smell dead people" and "I can see you." The crumbling building sat boarded up and vacant for years. Visitors saw a run-down, decaying brick edifice that even from the outside looked ominous and miserable. Inside, the building was just as foreboding and bleak. There was no longer anything to define it as a place where people went to get well. The building itself seemed to breathe despair. Gaping window frames and shattered glass still clung in jagged pieces at the corners, threatening anyone who dared to enter its gloom. Weathered packing boxes and crumbled newspapers were strewn about, and broken bottles and glass littered the floors. Doors hung from rusted hinges, flapping and creaking, and the sound of the wind whistled through the cracks. Paint peeled up in curls on walls and holes in the plaster, revealing rotted wood beneath. Bits of plaster and paint hung from ceilings that looked like they could come down any minute. The once-manicured lawn and weeds grew wildly around the faded and dirty brick structure, giving the whole building a hostile, unfriendly look. If they got enough nerve to go inside, visitors saw broken plaster, peeling paint, shutters hanging from windows and shards of glass. The smell of mildew permeated the air. The remains of upholstered chairs, ripped open with stuffing exposed to the elements, provided a home to families of mice and other vermin.

The remnants of its use as a mental hospital were said to have remained, including padded restraints hanging from the rafters. It is believed there was an underground tunnel leading directly to the morgue and an elevator that inexplicably had no doors to any of the floors. The attic was rumored to have contained several cages, the purpose of which is not known. While the entire building was said to be disturbing and forbidding, the basement was particularly so, with cold bursts of air, strange noises and disembodied voices filling the halls and footsteps and shadowing forms sweeping through rooms. People visiting the area at night have told of seeing orbs of light moving across the now vacant lot. Others, walking on or near the property, have heard whispering and moaning. Northshore was built as a place where people went to get rest and to recover and heal. The majority of people would have most likely recovered. However, where there is sickness, there is also sadness, anxiety, distress and sometimes even death. It is not known how many people died when the facility served as a sanatorium, as such records are sealed. But one would assume that a few did. It is also possible that someone died there when it was a mental hospital. The feelings of gloom and despair that people felt when they went inside the shuttered building could have been due to the condition of the building itself or the knowledge that it formerly served as a mental hospital. Perhaps the sadness and despair have left their imprints on the property, like an emotional photograph, and perhaps the departed souls who once wandered the sanatorium halls are now left to wander aimlessly across the land. While there is much here that could be of interest to paranormal investigators, the lot is currently fenced off. To date, no professional investigators have had the opportunity to explore the site. When and if they do venture there on a moonlit night, they may do well to be wary of the eyes that watch them from the dark.

9

CITY OF LOST SOULS

GHOSTS OF NUNICA CEMETERY

She clutches the teddy bear in her hand as she walks along the path. Suddenly, she sees a group of people ahead. Seeing a woman among them who looks kind, the little girl grabs her hand. Startled, the woman gasps as she feels an icy grip on her fingers and feels cold air that seems to go right through her. But no one is there. She is walking through Nunica Cemetery, and the little girl who gripped her hand is a ghost said to haunt it.

Nunica Cemetery, on Michigan Road 104, just off Cleveland Avenue, is known as the "City of Lost Souls." According to some people, it is one of the most haunted places in Michigan. Needless to say, it has become a popular destination for ghost hunters in recent years. Most cemeteries are peaceful places without a lot of ghostly goings-on, but Nunica Cemetery may be the exception to the rule. There are believed to be a number of restless spirits among the otherwise peaceful residents. These spirits, known by some as lost souls, have, on occasion, attempted to make themselves known to cemetery visitors in surprising ways. Paranormal investigators have picked up evoked voice phenomena from several of these spirits.

The village of Nunica, Michigan, was incorporated in 1872. Native Americans inhabited the area for centuries. The area was traveled by French-Canadian explorers early on as fur trappers made headway into the Michigan Territory. It is believed that Louis Jolliet and Father Jacques Marquette passed through the area in the eighteenth century. For many years, the only means of travel was by waterway. There were no roads to speak of. Traveling on foot was treacherous, owing to fallen timber, swamps and ravines. Even so, people did venture to the area. The first recorded white settler in Crockery Township was said to have been Manley Patchin, who came to the area in 1836. Manley later became a justice of the peace. Others soon followed. These early settlers were a hardy lot. That was a good thing, because the work of clearing land and preparing it for growing food was arduous. Most of the township's acreage was on state land, which the settlers were able to buy for about $1.25 an acre. Portions of the land were to be found on bounty warrants of soldiers from the War of 1812. These land grants were issued to officers and soldiers who had served for five years or more. When zinc was discovered near Crockery Creek, the population expanded quickly. The village's name comes from the Ottawan word *menonica*, which is what they called the clay from which they fashioned their earthenware. Crockery Creek, which meanders through the area, is believed to have been named for the broken Native American earthenware and pottery found along its banks.

In the early 1970s, three Native American mounds were discovered south of Nunica. When they were opened, they revealed a large number of skeletons, stone and copper tools and ornate earthenware vases. Some skeletal remains and relics close to the surface were occasionally dug up by plows in later years. In 1880, there were about one thousand people living in Nunica. After the zinc discovery, the area quickly experienced population growth as settlers came to work in the mines or to farm. Those who followed had a great impact on the growth of the village. Like Muskegon, a large part of its economy was lumber-based, although many of the pioneers combined farming with lumbering. As time went on and the lumber industry declined, many took to farming and raising stock. In those years, Nunica thrived as an agricultural haven, producing wheat, corn, butter, maple syrup, potatoes, fruit and other garden yields to serve the needs of its citizens. The arrival of Grand Trunk's railway connection between Grand Haven and Detroit further increased the population. In 1920, there were about eight thousand residents in Nunica. When the ore ran out in the late 1920s, the population declined drastically. The influenza epidemic that began in 1918 also had a devastating effect on Nunica; an outbreak in 1927 killed upward of eight hundred people, many of them children. By 1930, there were less than five thousand people living in Nunica. Another tragedy soon followed when lightning struck the train station in 1935. The resulting fire engulfed almost a third of the town. The train station was never rebuilt, sending the town's sustainability into free fall. By the late 1950s, there were fewer than one thousand citizens. The current population is about four hundred.

Nunica Cemetery, a secluded, quiet final resting place for Nunica's residents, was placed very near, or on top of, the Native American burial grounds. Established in 1883, the cemetery has been there since the beginning of the village. This spacious cemetery is well maintained, with manicured lawns. The site appears peaceful enough. The entire cemetery is silent. A tree-lined gravel road winds through this "city." Parts of the road are paved but are so weathered that large cracks line its surface. Large trees are present throughout the cemetery, overlooking many of the graves, like sentries protecting the city's inhabitants. Two enormous, twisted and gnarled trees near the entrance are scarred with graffiti and countless names. A man is rumored to have hanged himself from one of the trees. The tree appears to be missing a branch, said to have been removed in order to bring the body down. A few people have expressed a sense of unease when near the tree. A number of the graves are over one hundred years old and show signs of age. There are also newer headstones. There are numerous haphazardly placed, smaller grave markers, many so old that the names can no longer be read. One small cement sculpture, a lion, can be seen sitting quietly among the ferns and shrubbery. Many graves have been placed close together in groups, probably holding family members. A light covering of lichen mold is visible on the stones, giving them a gray-green appearance. Lichen often covers the ground as well as gravestones in older cemeteries. Urns hold artificial flowers brought by loved ones in remembrance. Veterans' graves are marked with flags and plaques. A few markers have coins placed on top to honor the memory of those buried below. The cement gravestones, many quite old, are pitted and mottled from time and weather.

Throughout its long history, there have been countless ghost stories involving the cemetery, about several ghosts in particular. One ghost is of a Civil War veteran who died in 1925. Another and more frequently sought-out ghost is that of the affectionate but shy Joel Bond. Joel was born in 1844 in Coopersville and died in 1923. This overly friendly apparition of the Civil War veteran has the reputation of being somewhat of a ladies' man. Women who venture too near Bond's grave will be subjected to having their hair played with or being touched on their bottoms. Bond's ghost is described as a dapper-looking, tall man in a suit and wearing a hat. The odor of cigar smoke can often be smelled near his grave site. There is one section of the cemetery where the children who died during the 1920 influenza epidemic were interred. This area seems to be the source of a significant amount of paranormal activity. Visitors or investigators in this section have felt a rush of cold air suddenly envelop them, only for the air

Headstone at Nunica Cemetery. Nunica, Michigan. *Photo courtesy of Darren Dykhouse, Lakeshore Paranormal. https://www.facebook.com/LakeshoreParanormal.*

to dissipate as quickly as it came. In other instances, their hands become freezing cold as if icy spectral fingers were gripping them. Mediums or empaths believe this to be the spirit of a little girl in need of comfort who grabs hold of people's hands. There is also the ghost of a small boy, around five or six years old, dressed in short pants with suspenders and a white shirt. He is often seen scampering among the grave markers playing hide-and-seek or sitting in a tree.

There are also stories of a little girl who appears to always carry something in her hand, either a teddy bear or a doll. Another familiar phantom resident is the "Lady in White." She appears wearing a flowing, flowery dress and floats silently over the grave markers. She will sometimes appear suddenly right next to visitors, startling them. Discarnate voices are often heard, one of a little boy. Other shadowy apparitions are felt more than seen, with people getting the upsetting feeling that they are being watched. In addition to Bond and the other apparitions, floating orbs are often seen flitting here and there. Electrical equipment or devices frequently malfunction. While most of the paranormal activity seems to happen at night, some people going into the cemetery during the day have noted a sense of apprehension or uneasiness. A few seasoned paranormal investigators have left the area as quickly as they arrived after getting an overwhelming feeling of dread, as if they were being warned off.

Paranormal investigator Candi Hess related an experience she and her husband had while visiting the Nunica Cemetery. She believed at that time that they had encountered the ghost of Joel Bond. She states:

> *A couple years ago the husband and I made a quick stop at Nunica Cemetery just at dusk. We didn't plan on staying long. He got out of the vehicle before I did...and was gone before I knew what way he went. I started walking towards a small hill in the drive....I stopped at the bottom 'cause I saw a figure standing at the top. I saw a man dressed in a uniform watching me. He then walked across the drive and walked into some bushes that were there. I felt dread...very uneasy. I knew I had to get out of there quick. So I turned around and started walking back to my vehicle. I heard footsteps coming up quickly behind me. When I reached the vehicle they stopped. My husband reached the vehicle about the same time....I told him we needed to leave and leave now. He asked why, and I told him what happened. He said he saw him too....He thought it was me at first until he saw my flashlight at the bottom of the hill. We got in the vehicle, and the only way out was to go up that hill. Which I told him he wasn't doing. So the only choice was to do a 100-point turnaround. He did, and we left. I was so unnerved about seeing Joel that day, I didn't go back there for weeks...and now I never go there past dusk. But now when I do go, I always stop to say hello to Joel.* [Candi Hess Facebook message, September 3, 2021.]

The City of Lost Souls has been investigated on many occasions, with high EMF readings being reported by investigators, although there are no electrical grids nearby. Power is said to quickly drain from cellphones and other electrical equipment when in the cemetery. Darren Dykhouse, of Lakeshore Paranormal, has investigated Nunica Cemetery no fewer than ten times—both during daylight hours and at night. Darren is always respectful when conducting investigations and attempting to communicate with any spirits present. In one visit, the investigators left flowers at the base of a tree as a peace offering. He has been able to pick up anomalous manifestations during many of these investigations. Darren says a lot of spirit activity happens there, including some he has experienced firsthand, from being grabbed by unseen hands to seeing a full-form apparition of a woman wearing a white dress. Distinct footsteps have been heard. People are said to be slapped by unseen hands, especially if they are being loud or obnoxious. On one investigation, he picked up EVP readings from a spirit named Mike, who seemed "pissed off." Darren got the distinct impression that Mike did not like him. Darren asked Mike if he had hanged himself there. A voice then came through on the device, saying, "3:12." Darren asked what happened at 3:12 but didn't get an answer. During another investigation, the EVP device picked up the sound of laughter, then a voice saying, "Joel...tell 'em...hello." They were asked if they were stuck there, to which the voice replied, "Unfortunately." Next, the name *Mark* was heard. When asked "Who is with us?," the reply was, "people" and "freaks. A final question was asked: "Are you a lost soul?" The voice answered, "lost."

These "Lost Souls," including Joel, Mike and the children, are the invisible people of Nunica Cemetery. Nevertheless, invisible people still have a story to tell. A few might seek help or comfort among the living, like the little girl ghost who just wants a hand to hold. Some are playful and prankish, like Joel, who likes to pinch the ladies, or the little boy who plays among the gravestones. Some souls, like Mike, want to be left alone and warn people off. This spiritual energy is what seems to draw empathic people like investigators and mediums to seek them out. Many ghosts just want their existence to be acknowledged. Some have stories to tell. This may be all that the spirits are looking for. After all, it may be nice to sit and listen to Joel Bond's war stories, learn about his life or hear if he had a lady friend; or play tag with a little boy ghost; or find out how to comfort the little girl with the teddy bear. If we could do these things, maybe these spirits would know that, even though they are no longer among the living, they are not lost.

10

Phantom Whispers and Flying Books

Ghosts of Hackley Library

Two women stood talking quietly in the library when an oddly dressed man noiselessly walked by. One of the ladies later recognized him as none other than the library's founder. She would have been delighted to speak with him—had he not disappeared into a wall. It may have been the ghost of Charles Hackley that she saw, still browsing the library's book-lined corridors. It's possible, if you believe in ghosts. Stories have circulated for years that the Hackley Library of Muskegon is haunted by none other than the ghost of its founder, philanthropist and lumbar baron Charles Hackley. The library, on Webster Avenue in Muskegon, was one of his first gifts to the city. Hackley Library has been a cornerstone of knowledge and community since its establishment. Hackley took great personal interest in the library in his lifetime. He was extremely vested in making Muskegon a vibrant community and continues to be one of the most respected and beloved lumber barons. There can be no doubt that the community at large has been greatly enriched by his interest in it, so it wouldn't be much of a stretch of the imagination to think that he continues to take an interest in what goes on here, even though he has passed over the veil.

After making his fortune in the lumber industry, Hackley devoted much time, effort and funds to uplift the community. He took great pleasure in bestowing gifts upon the city. The library was one of the first such gifts. Muskegon's first libraries were usually run by Sunday schools and contained only those books that were focused on religious or moral instruction of the young. Later library cooperatives and townships strived

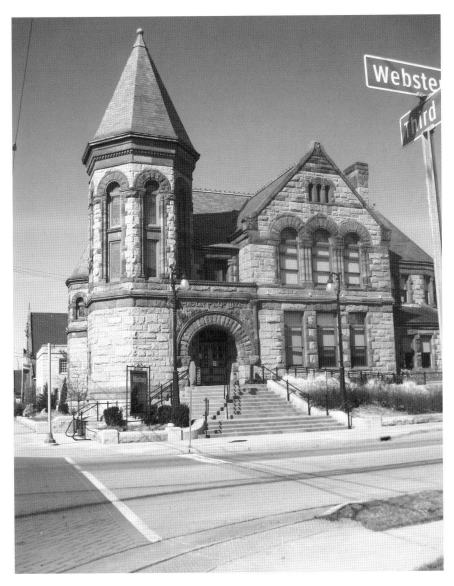

Hackley Public Library.

to provide books to public schools as best they could, although space was often limited, with books being relegated to storage areas. So Charles Hackley's gift of $100,000 to build a public library that would remain free to the public forever continues to be one of his most enduring and beloved endowments. Countless people both young and old continue to reap its benefits. It was Hackley's desire that the library be the cultural center of the city. But having a free library was a revolutionary idea for its time. The library was originally slated to cost around $50,000, but after finding the amount to be inadequate, Hackley donated another $25,000 for the purchase of books. The library was completed in October 1890. This stately Romanesque building, constructed of blue granite, is one of the most recognizable and iconic buildings in the city. An imposing turret, massive arched entrance, ornate woodworking and stained-glass windows are a few of its grand features. The lobby on the main floor is spacious and still has the original terra-cotta fireplace. Wood panels from the original circulation desk were kept after renovations in order to maintain the historic splendor. The main floor is reminiscent of a cathedral, with a towered ceiling and a rose-lined stairway winding through the turret. Several of the rooms are divided by elegant panes of glass with ornate door handles. Library patrons can read or study in this quiet, comforting space at the many roomy tables, browse movie and music titles or access the Internet on computers. The children's area has a vibrantly painted mural of fairy tales and other literary works to add to its charm. The Julia Hackley Reading Room holds the teen collections. Formerly the library reference room, it was later dedicated to Julia Hackley and is now used as a quiet reading room. A portrait of Julia hangs on the south wall facing a beautiful fireplace with a hand-carved mantelpiece. Casting a colorful glow over the main lobby are magnificent stained-glass windows featuring Mr. Hackley's favorite authors: Shakespeare, Goethe, Longfellow and William Hicklin Prescott. They have been restored to their original brightness and now radiate rays of light and warmth over the entire lobby. These dazzling panes were created by Louis Millet, the founder of an industrial art school and an interior designer. Another distinctive feature is the glass floor on the second floor. Made from six-inch clear glass, it is sturdy enough to hold the thousands of books and shelves that stand on it, in addition to library patrons. A few of the thick squares are a bit frosted over with age. There are narrow gaps between some squares that reveal the floor below. The first time stepping on it is a bit unnerving, but it is perfectly safe and really a remarkable experience once one gets used to it.

Over the years, numerous strange things are said to have occurred that had people believing the library had a few ghosts in residence, maybe even caused by the library's founder. Among the more recent peculiar things reported were books flying off a shelf. This happened on several occasions, once during a staff meeting, another time when a class was being held. The

Reading room, Hackley Library. *Based on original photo. Muskegon Picture Collection; Local History & Genealogy Dept., Hackley Public Library. Illustration by ©Gabe Schillman, www.GabeSchillman.com, 2022, Newaygo, Michigan.*

books didn't fall off the shelves—they flew across the room. One of the most astonishing incidents occurred when a library patron saw an apparition in Victorian clothing walk past her as she spoke to a staff member. This apparition then inexplicably disappeared into a wall. Later on, after seeing the painting of Mr. Hackley, she recognized him as being the same man she had seen disappear into the wall. Other patrons and workers have seen the reflection of a man dressed in similar clothing in a downstairs bathroom mirror. There have been occasions when people heard voices and other inexplicable sounds without finding an obvious source.

Needless to say, books flying off shelves of their own accord and apparitions in Victorian clothing appearing and disappearing into a wall are baffling and would certainly set one's nerves on edge. These incidents might fall under the category of the paranormal. One can also imagine how upsetting it would be for a woman or a girl to see the apparition of a man behind them while looking in a mirror while in the lady's room. A paranormal team was asked to investigate and

Above: Original fireplace in Julia Hackley Room, formerly the reading room, Hackley Library.

Opposite: Main floor of Hackley Library with a view of stained-glass windows featuring prominent Victorian-era writers.

find a cause for these mysterious incidents; their findings would then be presented at a seasonal event. Among the causes considered were telekinesis and psychokinesis, both of which are inexplicable by themselves and not always believed to exist. Both phenomena involve the spontaneous movement of objects through the air without any physical contact. These have been documented in other cases. One proposed explanation was that the books either fell or were pushed unbeknownst to the people sitting at a table in the library. To counter that theory, it was said that the books flew across the room as if thrown. Some of these incidents may have perfectly rational explanations; others may be more difficult to explain. Old buildings and houses creak and groan due to settling or old heating systems. Hearing people talking when no one is nearby may be the result of sound being carried from other floors. In fact, the library has stairwells that are closed off to the public. These are still sometimes used by library staff. This may account for the "discarnate" voices. What is more difficult to explain away is the apparition, dressed in the clothing of someone who lived one hundred years ago, disappear into solid walls and appear in mirrors. Most paranormal encounters manifest simply as noises, unusual smells, extreme cold or heat or the displacement of objects, so that would be quite alarming if encountered. In fact, even during investigations, it is quite rare to see any form of apparition, so the library sightings are noteworthy.

If it is Muskegon's beloved benefactor who is watching over the library, we have nothing to fear. Ghosts tend to become attached to familiar places, and there is no doubt that Charles Hackley was fond of his library. While there is no proof that the library is haunted by Mr. Hackley or any other ghost, these incidents are strange and a bit spooky. If it is Charles Hackley's ghost, it is completely in his character to be strolling through the book aisles, perhaps reading book titles as he goes along. Some have sensed a presence in the library, but no one has ever reported experiencing danger or malice. Hackley was a keen steward of his finances and took great pride and interest in his library. He contributed to its upkeep throughout his lifetime and left an endowment for its maintenance after his death. Consequently, it is not unlikely that he would want to continue keeping an eye on things. While a few people might find it unnerving or ridiculous that such a prominent ghost is walking around the library, others might find it comforting. To think that after all these years our founding father is still making sure that people are enjoying the literary wealth to be found in the library can make us feel good. Maybe this top-hatted ghost is Mr. Hackley, maybe not. After all, the library is such a storehouse of knowledge and entertainment that it would take more than one lifetime to get through it all. One can imagine Charles Hackley sitting in a comfortable chair, reading as he smokes a cigar, after everyone has gone home for the night. Perhaps he even reads ghost stories.

11

FOR HONOR AND COUNTRY

GHOST SAILORS OF LST 393

Working briskly and confidently, the crew slowed the engines to a standstill as they neared their destination. Within minutes, the cargo doors on the massive ship opened and the troops and equipment were unloaded onto the beach. Anticipation and anxiety were high. Hearts were pounding with fear and pride; the stakes couldn't have been higher. The beach was Omaha, and the day was June 6, 1944, D-Day. These were the men of USS Landing Ship Tank (LST) 393. The spirit of courage, honor and endurance they and thousands of others who served in the military embodied lives on through the memorabilia, stories and photographs on the decks of the LST 393 Veterans Museum in Muskegon, Michigan. While there is no doubt that their service to their country on that day should never be forgotten or taken lightly, some say the spirits of a few of the sailors who served aboard the LST 393 may still walk its decks. The USS LST 393 was a ship built for troop and equipment transport during World War II. It is now a museum moored at the Mart Dock in Muskegon. The museum hosts hundreds of visitors each year and has as its mission to preserve the ship's history, educate the public about its service during the war and honor American veterans. It hosts tours, programs and special events, including a D-Day reenactment. LST 393's place in history is unrivaled in its importance, and those who served on it deserve respect and remembrance. But there is a curious history connected to it. It is also rumored to be haunted. Among the reports are strange creaking, groaning and other noises when it is quiet. Some have reported feeling a presence on the ship, especially in certain areas. More inexplicable than the strange noises and feelings of a presence aboard is the reported sighting of an apparition.

The LST 393 is one of only two operational landing ship tanks known to exist. The LST 393, like the rest of the landing ship tanks, was powered by two diesel train engines that could also be manually steered with a stern rudder. Built in eighteen "Cornfield Navy" shipyards in Illinois, Indiana and Pennsylvania, these tough ships were constructed in just three years. Production increased from the initiation of the project. By 1945, it took only two months to manufacture an LST. The speed with which they were manufactured was in response to the need for combat vessels that could invade by sea. This massive wartime effort was one of the largest ship-building projects at the time.

While the men aboard these ships jokingly called them "Large Slow Targets," they were quite sturdy. Most of these LST ships survived the war, with only twenty-six losses in combat and only nine being sunk. They were originally designed during World War II to deploy troops, vehicles and supplies directly onto foreign beaches without using docks or cranes. They also helped to give the Allies the element of surprise during combat missions. The LST fleet was first used by the British during Operation Torch. The British realized their need for such ships after the defeat at Dunkirk in 1940, when needed equipment had to be left behind because there were no vessels able to transport it. Attempts were made to refit tankers. These efforts failed, so the United States was tasked with the redesign. Using the British concept, America took over production in 1941. Using a large ballast system, manufacturers were able to build a vessel that could cross the ocean as a deep-draft ship as well as maneuver onto beaches. LSTs were 328 feet long and 50 feet wide and could carry 2,100 tons. Cruising speed was 8.75 knots, with a maximum of 11.5 knots. The bow doors were 24 feet wide and could accommodate twenty-eight Sherman tanks or up to 385 fully equipped combat troops. The tanks could be moved onto the lower deck, with lighter vehicles, equipment and artillery loaded onto the upper deck by elevator. LSTs were built specifically for the war, and most of the American LST ships were armed with twenty-millimeter and forty-millimeter antiaircraft weapons. When the ships were empty, they could accommodate 500 troops and personnel. If carrying supplies, they could hold about 150 people. At the height of the conflict, they were in high demand throughout Europe and the Pacific. General Douglas McArthur employed them in the invasion of the Philippines. LSTs were also set up at

The USS LST 393 transported troops and equipment during World War II. LST 393 Veterans Museum. *Illustration by ©Gabe Schillman, www.studio37arts.com, 2022, Newaygo, Michigan.*

Allied forces D-Day reenactment, 2021. LST 393 Veterans Museum.

Above: D-Day reenactment, 2021. LST 393 Veterans Museum.

Opposite: LST 393 ship. LSTs were 328 feet long and 50 feet wide and could carry 2,100 tons. Their cruising speed was 8.75 knots, with a maximum of 11.5 knots. LST 393 Veterans Museum.

Iwo Jima and Okinawa, where they served in various capacities, including use as hospitals, for repairs and as ammunition ships. A few were outfitted with flight decks for small aircraft. More than one type of LST was produced, although some were used as transport or command ships and could not offload troops or supplies. It is no wonder that these ships played such an important role in World War II. LST 393 seemed to be at the top of that list.

The LST 393 was first launched on November 11, 1942, and commissioned on December 11. Lucy Sorenson was a sponsor at its launching. The ship's first commanding officer was USNR Commander Lieutenant John H. Halifax. LST 393 was active in three invasions and made more than seventy-five voyages, including stops in Italy, the British Isles, France, North Africa and the Canal Zone, covering over fifty-one thousand nautical miles. The ship was awarded service medals and three battle stars on the European, African and Middle Eastern fronts. LST 393's extensive and extraordinary military campaigns included major roles in Sicily, Italy; the invasion of Normandy in 1944 at Omaha Beach; the liberation of the Philippines; and the capture of Iwo Jima and Okinawa. The campaigns seemed to go nonstop and at breakneck speed from country to country. On June 6, 1944, at the invasion of Normandy, after offloading war materials and Sherman tanks, LST 393 was trapped for several days.

Armored tank. D-Day reenactment, 2021. LST 393 Veterans Museum.

The *1944 War Diary* reported that on June 5, 1944, the LST 393 was moored at Falmouth Harbor in Falmouth, England, when it was signaled from a flag ship to weigh its anchor. The ship was underway at 0823 hours and joined a convoy, Task Group 126.4, and it commenced operation plan 1-44. From that day until June 21, the ship saw plenty of action. On June 7, a convoy of LSTs and numerous other ships left Falmouth headed to Colleville, France, carrying personnel and equipment. They anchored just off the Fox Green section of Omaha Beach, bringing aboard 1,135 casualities. On June 8, general quarters was sounded. With enemy planes overhead, the fleet held its fire. The ships weighed anchor at 1515 and were underway to get closer to the beach. They let the stern anchor go at 1531 at Baie de la Seine off Colleville. Men from LST 75 were on board the LST 393 for transfer, and 2,025 casualties were taken aboard. The LST 393 got underway again and proceeded to North Bound, Anchorage, where they joined other LSTs making their way to Portland, England. On

Armored tank, "Smoky," and troops at D-Day reenactment, 2021. LST 393 Veterans Museum.

Armored tank, D-Day reenactment, 2021. LST 393 Veterans Museum.

LST-393 ship gun. Most of the American ships were armed with twenty-millimeter and forty-millimeter antiaircraft weapons. LST-393 Veterans Museum.

Allied troops, D-Day reenactment. LST 393 Veterans Museum.

Allied troops, D-Day reenactment. LST 393 Veterans Museum.

June 13, the LST 393 was headed back to Colleville and weighed anchor at Utah Beach. Two days later, it joined a convoy and made their way to Southampton and took 1,137 casualties aboard.

On June 16, the LST 393 joined a convoy to beach at Baie de la Seine in Colleville. It set anchor and proceeded to get closer to the beach, anchoring off Omaha at Fox Red beach. On June 17, 1944, the ship weighed anchor at Dog White Beach. General quarters was sounded after the reception of a red alert, but the ship didn't come under fire. The crew was secured from general quarters and began unloading personnel and vehicles. LST 393 then received orders from HMS *Ceres* to proceed on to Portland, England, with LCT 210 in tow. On June 18, LST 393 joined a convey to Omaha and Utah Beaches at Baie de la Seine, beaching on the "S" Red Section of Utah Beach. The crew began unloading vehicles and personnel. After that, the ship took aboard casualties and survivors from the beach. On June 20, it proceeded to HMS *Ceres* for further instructions. The LST 393 weighed anchor again off Omaha Beach at the southeast end of the Kansas Light Ship at Baie de la Seine after having to maneuver around a storm. The ship moved on with a convoy headed for Southampton, with LST 393 acting as the commodore. On June 21, with a pilot aboard, it moored in Southampton Harbor in Southampton, England. The crew unloaded casualties before reloading the ship with British army vehicles, troops, officers and other personnel.

During its exemplary wartime service, the LST 393 transported over 9,100 soldiers and 3,248 vehicles, including howitzers, jeeps and tanks. It also transported over 5,000 prisoners of war and over 800 casualties, both American and Allied. There is no doubt that the entire fleet of landing ship tanks played a vital role in securing peace. However, after the war, there was no longer a need for them, although a few were in service up until the Vietnam era. Of the 1,051 landing ship tanks constructed, half were sold as scrap, some sold to commercial enterprises or foreign countries, a few were sunk and several went into private use. The LST 393 was decommissioned on March 14, 1947. It was eventually sold and renamed Highway 16 as part of a waterway extension of U.S. Highway 16 from Detroit to Muskegon, ferrying automobiles. In 2000, efforts were begun to purchase the aging ship. It was brought to Muskegon, coming up the Mississippi River to our port, where it sat, languishing and in sore need of repair for many years. Efforts to revitalize it were slow, but through the efforts of several groups, the ship was restored to its former glory in order to memorialize and honor those who served. The museum houses thousands of artifacts, photos and memorabilia such as scrapbooks and keepsakes, giving visitors a personal view into the lives of these veterans. The walls are lined with photographs of the men and women who served in all branches of the military, as well as depictions of what life was like on the ship.

A self-guided tour of LST 393 shows there are six decks, five of which are open to the public. The main deck is the tank deck. One display that stands out is a glass case holding the actual battle flag flown over LST 393 when it landed on Omaha Beach on D-Day. Another poignant display on the back wall shows photographs and service history of the sixty servicemen from the Muskegon area who were killed in action. The next level is the

LST 393 moored at Mart Dock. LST 393 Veterans Museum.

berthing deck, where combat troops slept. Two decks below this is the engine room, where the Sperry Gyro-Compass, which was used to help navigate the ship, still stands. The officers' and captain's quarters were on the top deck, near the navigation bridge. The officers' deck was off-limits to enlisted men. Officers' rooms had real mattresses on the beds instead of the no-frills rack-tape beds for enlisted personnel. The galley was where the enlisted men stood in the chow line for meals. Making meals for that many men was an arduous task for a cook aboard an LST. There were 13 cooks working three shifts, serving a crew of 36 officers, 250 enlisted men and 250 other complementary personnel, such as tank drivers and soldiers. The mess deck was where the enlisted men ate in shifts. Officers ate in the ward room, where they could sit at tables with their meals served by stewards. Four hatches led out to the weather deck. During the war, the ship had fifty-caliber Mark 4 antiaircraft guns and twenty-millimeter antiaircraft cannons on board as well as other combat equipment. Much of the smaller equipment was brought up by elevator. The center of the deck held the navigating bridge deck, radio room and chart room, where the ship's course was plotted. Through the chart room is the wheelhouse, or pilothouse. This was where much of the operation was controlled. The captain's quarters were under the wheelhouse. This level also held the sick bay, where medical problems were handled. The wounded were passed on stretchers up to the sick bay through a narrow horizontal door that opened onto the tank deck, saving men from having to carry patients up the stairs.

With so many artifacts from World War II, as well as other wars, it is possible that there is a spirit that has become attached to something on board, or a "trigger object." These trigger objects—memorabilia, personal effects, uniforms, objects the sailors used, as well the places they frequented—are believed by paranormalists to draw the spirits to them, keeping them "stuck." If so, then there is much here that would serve as attachments. These are the bits and pieces of the men's daily lives, things they felt important or that they used frequently, where they slept and what they experienced. If an object does have an attachment, it might be felt by empaths or picked up on instrumentation. While no particular object was suspected of having an attachment, several investigations were conducted by area paranormal investigators who hoped to shed some light on these stories. On October 4, 2019, a group of paranormal investigators gathered on board LST 393, located at the Mart Dock in Muskegon. The groups included: GRASPP, Kent County Paranormal, Lakeshore Paranormal and the Michigan Area Paranormal Investigative Team. The investigation

Above: LST 393 enlisted men's quarters. Equipment picked up EVP activity in this area. LST 393 Veterans Museum.

Opposite: Officers' dining area. LST-393 Veterans Museum.

lasted three hours. During the course of the investigation, the investigators were able to capture some significant energy fields and activity with their instruments. The investigation started with a walk-through guided by a member of the museum staff. At one point, they were shown a table that doubled as an operating table and the area where the injured were brought up to surgery. They then walked through the crew's quarters. At one point, murmurs were picked up on EVP in the engine room. They also received a lot of positive interactive responses from the spirit realm, which Darren was able to capture on video. Someone asked, "How many spirits are with us?" A voice was captured replying "three." When the question was asked, "How many people were here?," the captured response was "nine." There were six people in the room. With the three spirits, there were nine.

The Kent County Paranormal Group was in the engine room when one of the team reportedly saw a full-form apparition of a man in the corner of the room. Darren, of Lakeshore Paranormal, went back to see if he could communicate with the form. After the spirit was asked to make a noise, they heard a loud "click." They left a sensor and invited him to touch it so they would know he was there. They also checked for any spikes in energy on EVP. Darren walked through quietly, trying to pick up any energy, and he then turned on his necrophonic app. The app immediately began

LST 393 engine room. A full-form apparition was seen in the back section of the room.
LST 393 Veterans Museum.

picking up snippets of phrases and words in short bursts. While some were undecipherable, at other times the eerie metallic voice reverberating in the darkened room was chillingly distinct. Darren also picked up anomalous activity during a walk-through of the shower area. While in the lavatory, they could hear someone walking behind them, but when they turned around to look, no one was there. Dan, of Kent County Paranormal, picked up a lot of EVP activity. A shadowy form was also reportedly seen by investigators in the main part of the ship and on the mezzanine. The figure could be seen moving quickly up and down the stairs. In one area, a sign overhead flashed, "Report to your stations." After Brandon asked where they were supposed to go if the light flashed, the lights suddenly started flashing as if in response. One common complaint in the military is the food. This idea might have prompted one team member to ask if the food was any good when they were in the galley area. The EVP picked up "no" and "help me." Apparently, bad food is something one will remember, even in the afterlife. A sad presence was sensed in one of the officers' quarters. Investigators were able to pick up EVP signals there. While standing near the ship's wheel, Brandon Hoezee

The author standing by *Bugle Boy of Company B* in front of LST-393 Veterans Museum, 2018. It commemorates Muskegon native Clarence Zylman, a prominent bugler who promoted boogie-woogie music. It was sculpted by Ari Norris. LST 393 Veterans Museum. Muskegon, Michigan. *Photo by Raven Rae Lockhart.*

reported a spirit voice eerily whispering "I am watching you" in his ear. It was at that point that the group descended to the engine room.

Whether or not you believe that ghostly sailors walk LST 393, first and foremost to be remembered is that the vessel serves as a memorial to the lives of the men and women who served so valiantly. It may give comfort to think they are with us, protecting us still. Coming aboard this ship museum as a visitor and being surrounded by the artifacts and memorabilia and learning the stories and history of LST 393 can be a very powerful and overwhelming experience. Even if there are no ghosts present, the connection to these men is real. How they fought, how they lived and how they perished is understood not just by reading and looking at the artifacts; it can also be felt. Walking through the ship, all the emotions they experienced—loss, sadness, despair, happiness and hope—become real. While it is obvious that there is something unusual and a bit mysterious about LST 393, if there are ghost sailors walking its decks, we should also remember how vital this ship was to the world in some of its darkest days. This museum continues to stand as a living testament to those who served and the sacrifices they made.

12

CURSE OF THE *GRIFFON*

LAKE MICHIGAN'S FIRST GHOST SHIP

The skies were obscured by threatening clouds. The wind quickly picked up and whipped the lake into a fury, rocking the small craft boats that dotted the surface. Suddenly gliding silently over the choppy waves, a ship slowly came into view, unlike anything the boaters had ever seen. With a wooden bow curled up almost like a shoe, massive sails that billowed in the wind and a giant mythical creature on its mast, it was like something out of a fairytale. As they watch incredulously, the wraithlike vessel passed by them, seemingly floating above the water. There was no captain or crew in sight. Then, just as inexplicably as it arrived, it disappeared into the mist. If the boaters knew their maritime lore, they would surely know that this was none other than the *Griffon* appearing to warn them of danger. Throughout maritime history, there have been countless stories told by sailors of ghost ships, many said to sail the Great Lakes. However, the *Griffon* is one ghost ship that has almost been lost to time. But it is no less mysterious or intriguing. The *Griffon* (the name means "protection against fire") was built by ex-priest and French explorer René-Robert Cavelier, Sieur de La Salle. La Salle was one of the earliest explorers in North America and is believed to be the first European to trek across the interior of Michigan. At the time, the colonies were still unexplored wilderness, and much of the area was unchartered. Canada and the Northwest Territory were known as "New France." La Salle was born in 1643 in Rouen, France. He immigrated to North America from Montreal, Canada, where he farmed and traded in furs. In addition to farming and the fur trade, La Salle was interested in finding a faster route to China. At the time, the only known path was around Africa, which was a long and treacherous venture. La Salle believed a passage could be found through North America after the Iroquois told him of a large river located in the interior. This river flowed west, which La Salle knew to be the same direction as China. In 1669, he and his party sailed down the Saint Lawrence River by canoe to Lake Ontario and then went by land. La Salle explored North America for most of his life. He had also amassed a large fortune by trade with Native Americans. While La Salle never found a new trade route to China, much knowledge of North America was gained, and his trade relationship with Native Americans helped to bolster Native American and French ties. La Salle owned three ships but needed one that could withstand the rigors of traversing the Great Lakes. Storms on these lakes were known to be brutal and weather conditions unpredictable. The *Griffon* was the first large ship to sail Lakes Erie, Huron and Michigan. Before this, they had only been navigated by canoe. Navigating Niagara Falls was impossible, thus the *Griffon* was built above the falls in the Niagara River near Count Frontenac. It was launched near Cayuga Island. It is not known exactly what the ship looked like, but an early woodcut rendition showed a two-masted ship. Research reveals it was more likely a one-masted barque with square sails, thirty to forty feet in length with a ten- to fifteen-foot beam. In any case, it was the largest vessel then known to sail those lakes.

Much of the *Griffon*'s maiden—and final—voyage has been documented and has become a well-known part of Michigan and U.S. history. La Salle and a crew of thirty-four set sail on August 7, 1679, near Niagara Falls. They navigated using a mapping chart made ten years earlier by René de Galinées, an explorer and Native American missionary. Also on board was Father Louis Hennepen. They went west on Lake Erie to the Detroit River, passing through what was later named Lake St. Clair. In order to get the ship across to Lake Huron from Erie, it was pulled by ropes over the rapids, up the Saint Clair River, then into Lake Huron. They sailed north into Saginaw Bay, where they were forced to make port, as there was not enough wind. They were able to set sail again on August 15, this time with La Salle piloting. Unfortunately, they encountered a violent storm and had to lower their sails to prevent the ship from floundering. This left them at the mercy of the current. They were adrift until August 27, when they again picked up a good headwind. They arrived at an area near Saint Ignace, Michigan, and weighed anchor at a natural harbor on Mackinac Island. Over one hundred

Huron and Ottawa Native Americans, who had gathered to trade fur pelts, greeted La Salle and his crew. After leaving Mackinac Island, the ship went on to Green Bay, Wisconsin, with a crew of six, carrying thousands of dollars in furs. They made port near Rock Island, Wisconsin, where there was a settlement of Ottawan and Huron Native Americans, a few Frenchmen and fifteen fur traders that La Salle had sent ahead. The fur traders had collected over twelve thousand pounds of pelts waiting for the *Griffon*. The plan was to take the pelts back to Niagara and return with supplies. La Salle stayed behind. The ship was never seen again. When the ship failed to return, La Salle and five others went overland by foot, back to Niagara. In doing so, they became the first Europeans to travel across the interior of Michigan.

In addition to being Michigan's first ghost ship, the *Griffon* is considered the "Holy Grail" of Great Lakes shipwrecks. One couple who say they have found the wreck of the *Griffon* after 350 years is Steve and Kathie Libert. The wreckage of a ship about the size and shape of the *Griffon* was discovered near Poverty Island, but due to legal wrangling between the State of Michigan, France and shipwreck hunters, efforts to do further exploration have been stymied. Using historical documents as well as other research, the Liberts believe the wreckage near Poverty Island is, in fact, the *Griffon* in its final resting place.

The disappearance of the *Griffon*, like thousands after it, was chalked up to being the victim of a typical storm, but Lake Michigan is anything but typical. Like the other Great Lakes, it is enigmatic and deadly, especially for the unwary. The Great Lakes are privy to rogue storms, anomalous weather conditions that have resulted in thousands of ship disappearances since the *Griffon* first set course. Even so, these conditions may not account for some of the mysterious and sudden disappearances or sinking of so many ships. Since the maiden voyage of the *Griffon*, anywhere from six thousand to eight thousand ships are known to have met disaster on the Great Lakes. Some believe many of these disappearances or wrecks are due to bad luck in attempting to travel though an area known as the Michigan Triangle. This mysterious span of water seems to have claimed more ships and lives than the Bermuda Triangle. The Bermuda Triangle is an area in the Atlantic Ocean near the southern coast of the United States where numerous ships, aircraft and people are said to have vanished without a trace. What is more inexplicable is that some of the ships are reported to have actually reappeared, minus the people or any remains of them. How this could happen, if true, is beyond the ken of modern science. The Michigan Triangle includes Manitowoc, Wisconsin; Ludington, Michigan;

and Benton Harbor, Michigan. Encompassed within this triangle is a good portion of the lake, with ships coming from ports along the lake to cross its lines. The *Rouse-Simmons*, or the "Christmas tree ship," may have also fallen victim to the triangle.

For the most part, Lake Michigan is a pretty calm body of water, but its mood can change at a moment's notice, with sudden squalls and high winds that can buffet about ships or pull swimmers beneath the waves in treacherous undertows. Lake Michigan is the only Great Lake entirely within U.S. boundaries and has features more fitting to an ocean than a lake. It is about 280 feet deep (about 920 feet at the deepest portion), with 1,640 miles of shoreline. In addition to its changeable nature and weather, the bottom hides another curiosity that some say is the cause of many shipwrecks and volatile lake conditions. Within its depths lie anomalous stone structures arranged in a circle that some call the Michigan Stonehenge. These structures were discovered in 2007 and have yet to be fully investigated. More baffling than the stone circle is a large stone with what appears to be a mastodon situated at the center of this circular formation. Mastodons roamed the Great Lakes region about twelve thousand years ago and have long since disappeared, so if the carving is man-made, it dates back many thousands of years. It is suggested that this "Stonehenge" is the source of the odd weather patterns, strange disappearances and shipwrecks that have occurred since at least the 1800s.

There are many theories as to what happened to the *Griffon*. Some believe the crew sank the boat and took the furs. Others believe that the Seneca, who had been suspicious of this monstrous ship and had made several attempts to burn it, succeeded. Some have postulated that they placed a curse on it. The Seneca and Iroquois tribes feared the ship, believing its creation threatened the "Great Spirit." A legend states that an Iroquois prophet, Metiomek, placed a curse on the *Griffon* and La Salle, telling him that darkness would overcome him and the ship, that it would sink and that La Salle's blood would be on the hands of those he trusted. Another theory is that the Jesuits had something to do with its disappearance. La Salle believed that the men mutinied, stole the furs and sank the ship. While the theories are intriguing, most modern-day researchers believe the ship sank after getting caught in a storm. The curse seems to have come to pass, as the ship disappeared into the depths of the lake. La Salle was murdered by a mutinous crew member several years later.

At this point, it is uncertain if the Poverty Island wreckage is the *Griffon*, but the *Griffon* holds historical significance in any case, both as local history and as American history. Although the remains of the *Griffon* may rest in the depths of Lake Michigan, it is believed that its spirit and the spirits of the men on board do not. Maybe Metiomek's curse still dooms these spirits. A Native American legend relates that the *Griffon* and its crew are doomed to traverse the lake as ghosts. The sound of the men's eerie voices calling out can be heard as the ship sails gloomily in the mist. Stories of the phantom ship have been passed down through the years by boaters, anglers and others. Like many other ship apparitions, the sight of the *Griffon* is believed to portend treacherous weather conditions and is a warning to stay off the lake. Interestingly, one group diving near the Poverty Island wreckage reported a sense of foreboding and unease as soon as they came near it. Mundane explanations are often found to explain such sightings, from optical illusions made by weather conditions and mirages. However, paranormal explanations should not be discounted. So, if you are ever out on a boat on a moonless night and see the *Griffon*'s frightful bow piercing through the mists, know it is time to head for port.

13

DEAD MAN'S HAND

CENTURY CLUB GHOST

If he was a gambling man, he would have probably bet it all on the cards he held in his hand that night. He would have won big. What he couldn't have known is that the stakes were worth more than money. Had he known, he would have chosen to walk away that night. Such life-and-death decisions can haunt the living. Maybe they can even haunt the dead. A man named Frank got dealt the wrong hand one day long, long ago, and now his spirit is believed to haunt the Century Club. The club, another of Muskegon's historic buildings, is rumored to be haunted by an unlucky card-playing ghost by the name of Frank. Not much is known about Frank, other than that he and a group liked to play cards in the basement. He may or may not have been a Century Club member. The club was a popular means of social interaction, especially before the age of radio, television and the Internet. Many of these clubhouses were reserved for the well-to-do, and usually only for men. It was a means of sharing ideas, networking, camaraderie and checking on the news of the day. This socializing and networking included playing games like cards. Although playing poker and gambling were against the rules of the Century Club and against the law, it's possible that a few adventurous men occasionally flaunted those rules.

The Century Club began as the Muskegon Club in March 1887. At its start, there were 190 members, all men, who socialized and played games such as whist, pool and billiards. Later, it was decided to open the club to women on certain days and hours. In 1981, memberships were opened to include members' wives. Members paid a monthly fee of $15, or $300 for a lifetime membership. At its start, the Muskegon Club had no permanent meeting place and was renting space at the opera house. The group considered multiple options for future growth. Club member John Torrent proposed the construction of a permanent clubhouse that would combine a meeting house with retail shops, and a site was suggested between Clay and Second Avenues. Plans moved forward, the only change being that a hotel would occupy the lower level instead of shops. The plan changed again when the club broke with Torrent, who resigned his membership. Members then opted to go with L.G. Mason's idea to build the club on Western Avenue, and once again construction moved forward. Mason, along with lumber barons A.V. Mann and G.C. Hills, were on the building committee. Games were a vital aspect of the clubhouse, and the group originally planned to have bowling and billiards in the basement, with card games and reading rooms on the upper floors. A ballroom was planned for the top floor.

Fictionalized representation of the ghost of Frank standing at the bar with other Century Club members, 2022. *Illustration by ©Gabe Schillman, www.studio37arts.com, Newaygo, Michigan.*

The building, designed by Sidney Osgood of Grand Rapids, is made of red brick and tiles with the focal point being its arched stone entrance. The interior of the building is red oak, with pinewood in the basement. The arch, with striking ornamental grillwork, overlooks a wide cement stairway. This entrance leads directly into a long hallway that extends the entire length of the main floor. On the right were two large parlors that took up the majority of this floor that were connected by a sliding door. The front parlor served as a reception area, and the second was the banquet parlor, near the back of the building. To the left was a reading room that overlooked the street below. A staircase immediately on the left led to the second floor. Another staircase went down to the basement. The back of the building held an office and storage room. Behind the storage room were three card rooms. There were hallways connecting these rooms and to the banquet parlor. Most of the second-story space was made up of divided parlors, some divided only by curtains. The club moved into the building in January 1889, with a gala reception held soon after. This was an elegant affair, with over three hundred guests attending. The local newspaper heralded the event, giving a detailed account for those not in attendance. Local press published descriptions of ladies dressed in bejeweled finery and men dressed to the nines in tuxedos and top hats. The mantels, chandeliers and stairways were lushly garlanded with red and white carnations, roses and ferns. A flower arrangement spelling out the monogram of the club was a centerpiece. An orchestra was on hand for entertainment and dancing. The festivities also included card games, billiards and bowling. The banquet room was later opened, and a sumptuous selection of refreshments was served by Occidental Hotel staff. The reception continued well into the night. It was a luxurious event. Needless to say, it was the talk of the town for many days.

The club closed in 1901 for repairs and renovations. A new billiard table was installed, as were flooring, new furniture and carpeting. The bowling lanes, one of the club's most popular features, were upgraded to standard length. The clubhouse was then reopened as the Century Club. When the club's mortgage was paid off in 1945, another large gala was held, with a lavish dinner, drinks and games. The building was remodeled again in 1949. By then, there were about four hundred members. Membership grew to around five hundred by the 1950s. In 1974, when the Muskegon Mall was being constructed, the building was connected to the mall but remained outside the mall structure proper. The clubhouse was remodeled again in 1981. The renovation included

Century Club building. The ghost of Frank is said to haunt the basement.

several new dining rooms, kitchens, a bar, a dance floor and a library. But like all good things, the games, events and good times at the clubhouse ended. After one hundred years in operation, the Century Club closed permanently in 1991. With its demise, the lavish receptions, bowling, billiards and card games became little more than memories. However, its importance as a part of Muskegon history lives on. When the mall was being demolished, the club was saved from destruction because of its historic significance. The building was again renovated and new life breathed into its hallowed halls. Ironically, it seemed to take on a purpose similar to what John Torrent envisioned at its beginning. The building is home to a variety of boutiques and shops that became the Century Club Retail Center. The ballroom was reopened as an event venue. The basement now houses an arts center.

It is said that the basement is where the ghost of Frank has made a few unexpected appearances since he got dealt a lethal hand. If he had known it was to be his last game, he may have picked something a little less exciting, like Go Fish or whist. Whist, a popular Victorian-era game, did not have the same pizazz or stakes as poker, especially if participants were playing for money. The story goes that a group of men were playing poker in the basement, a man named Frank among them. One night, Frank got the best and rarest hand of all: A royal flush. This hand comprises the ten, jack, queen, king and ace of the same suit. If you have never played cards, you should know that the odds of getting a royal flush are astronomically low. How rare is this hand? Statistically, the odds are 2,598,960 to 1, or 0.00015 percent. This hand is so rare that if you played cards every night for eighty-nine years, you would probably get to hold only one such hand. Nobody has that kind of time. Nobody knows how often Frank played cards or for how many years. That night, the odds were with him, or so he thought. Frank was undoubtedly excited at his luck. There was no way he could have held a poker face with a hand like that. But his good luck didn't last. As he placed his hand on the table to show his cards, his excitement got the better of him. He became so overwrought that he had a heart attack and slumped over the table, his cards splayed out across the table. To the utter shock and horror of his poker buddies, Frank died right there at the table. Fate had played its hand. If the group was playing for money, Frank never got the chance to collect on his bet.

Over the years, Frank's ghost is said to make his presence known in certain areas of the building, usually the basement. Frank may be looking to collect his winnings or trying to find some new poker buddies. If so, they should be careful not to get too excited if they get a royal flush, least they cash in their chips, like poor Frank did. No one would want the hand that Frank was dealt if they knew it would be their last. Frank may have started a new version of the "dead man's hand" around town. There was a similarity between the two hands. In both, someone ended up dead. Historically, the "dead man's hand" is two aces and two eights. Getting a pair of anything is not that bad in poker, especially if no wild cards are allowed. It's not at all unusual. Winding up dead, however, is strange. This hand goes all the way back to the Old West and the famous lawman whose name will always be associated with it. The story goes that Wild Bill Hickok was holding a pair of aces and eights when he was shot dead at the poker table on August 2, 1876, at Nuttal and Man's Saloon in Deadwood in the Dakota Territory. Being dealt aces and eights has been synonymous with death ever since that fateful day. It is a story still told at poker tables around the world. Frank may not have been holding aces and eights that day, but his luck had run out, as had Wild Bill's.

EPILOGUE

Muskegon's history is a long one, going back several hundred years at the very least. So it is no wonder that we have countless stories that are ripe with mystery and wonder. Many of these stories have yet to be told. If spirits dwell among us, then perhaps we should welcome them, as they might reveal a resilient and tough pioneering spirit. Muskegon is a strong city with a willingness to do what it takes to grow and prosper. From the fur trappers, lumber barons and settlers who came here from all over to a multicultural, unique and growing community, Muskegon continues to thrive, and its resilient, pioneering spirit lives on. Try as some skeptics and naysayers might, the paranormal cannot be dismissed out of hand. There are too many credible accounts and witnesses of inexplicable events to do so. To say it is all faked, fiction or illusion is to ignore a multitude of evidence. The mysterious facets of life, death and the hereafter covered by the veil have always been with us. However, the veil may be lifting. More and more people are questioning what lies beyond. Paranormal investigators, mediums, psychics, empaths and ghost hunters may be the ones to find the answers to some age-old questions. Until that day, we will continue to seek, to learn and to keep an open mind. It may be that sometime in the near future, we will know for certain the true nature of these hauntings and the definitive answer to the question: Are ghosts real?

Hume House under a full moon, 2022. *Painting by ©Gabe Schillman, www.studio37arts.com, Newaygo, Michigan.*

BIBLIOGRAPHY

Access Genealogy. "Ottawa Tribe." Accessed February 16, 2021. https://
  accessgenealogy.com.
Alexander, Dave. "Century Club Center Returns to Its Historic Roots with
  New Gathering Hall." *Muskegon Chronicle*, February 19, 2012. Accessed
  August 9, 2021. https://www.mlive.com/news/Muskegon.
Angelo, Lyna D., and Bill Moore. "Charles Henry Hackley." Welcome to
  the Lighthouse. Accessed July 19, 2021. https://freepages.rootsweb.
  com/~muskegoncounty/genealogy.
Bourrie, Mark. "Witch of November: The Cruel Month that Has Seen
  Many Great Lakes Sailors Perish beneath the Waves." *National Post*,
  November 12, 2013. https://nationalpost.com.
Brouwer, Emily. "Lumber Baron's Families' Deaths, Obituaries Highlighted
  During Tours." Michigan Live, May 21, 2019. https://www.mlive.com.
Capps, Chris. "The Navaho Ghost Sickness." Unexplanable.net. January
  7, 2012. https://www.unexplainable.net.
Caribbean-Pirates. "Myths and Superstitions of Pirates and Sailors."
  Accessed May 24, 2021.https://caribbean-pirates.com.
Center for Michigan History Studies. "Biography: Charles Hackley.
  Accessed August 2, 2021. http://www.michigan-history.org.
———. "A Brief History of Lumbering in Michigan." Accessed February
  15, 2021. http://www.michigan-history.org.

Chaffin, Sean. "The History of Dead Man's Hand and How to Play it."
888poker.com, emagazine, November 11, 2019. https://www.888poker.
com/magazine/poker-world/dead-mans-hand Accessed August 10,
2021.

Christina. "Connecting with Spirits Using Dowsing Rods." Psychic Scoop,
September 20, 2016. https://www.psychicscoop.com.

City Data. "Muskegon, Michigan." Accessed May 12, 2021. https://www.
city-data.com.

City of Muskegon. "A Brief History of Public Health in Muskegon
County. A Historical Perspective." March, 2003. Accessed August 11,
2021. https://co.muskegon.mi.us.

Clash of the Cultures in 1910s and 1920s. "Image and Lifestyle." Accessed
October 27, 2021. https://ehistory.osu.edu.

———. "The New Woman." Accessed October 27, 2021. https://ehistory.
osu.edu.

———. "Work, Education, and Reform." Accessed October 27, 2021.
https://ehistory.osu.edu.

Craven, Jackie. "Queen Anne Architecture in the U.S.A., Reigning Style
of America's Industrial Age." ThoughtCo, July 3, 2019. https://www.
thoughtco.com.

Davis, Susan B., trans. "Nunica." *Coopersville Observer*, August 21, 1931.
Migenweb.org. Accessed August 20, 2021. http://www.migenweb.org.

Diane and Kelly, hosts. "Haunted Cemeteries 16, Episode 356." *History
Goes Bump*. Podcast. 29:03. October 15, 2020. Accessed August 20, 2021.
http://historygoesbump.com.

Dykhouse, Darren. "LST 393 Investigation, Paranormal Equipment
and Investigative Methods." Lakeshore Paranormal. Facebook group.
https://www.facebook.com. Personal interview with author. April 4,
2021.

———. "Oakwood and Nunica Cemeteries." Lakeshore Paranormal.
Facebook group. www.facebook.com. Personal interview with author.
April 21, 2021.

———."USS LST 393 Paranormal Investigation UNCUT." Youtube.com.
Lakeshore Paranormal. August 29, 2020. Video, 1:03:38. Accessed June
8, 2021. www.youtube.com.

Eckert, Kathryn Bishop. "Frauenthal Center for the Performing Arts
(Michigan Theater, Muskegon, Michigan)." Society of Archicectural
Historians. 2012. Last accessed February 11, 2021. http://sah-
archipedia.org.

Family Search. "U.S. War of 1812 Bounty Land Warrants." Accessed August 24, 2021. https://www.familysearch.org.

Find a Grave. "Joel A. Bond (1844–1913)." Memorial ID 11616368, citing Nunica Cemetery, Nunica, Ottawa County, Michigan, USA. Maintained by Megan Heyl. Accessed August 20, 2021. https://www.findagrave.com.

Genealogy Trails. "Muskegon County Miscellaneous News Stories." Accessed February 20, 2021. http://genealogytrails.com.

GeogMich. "The French Fur Trade." Accessed February 18, 2021. https://project.geo.msu.edu.

Good Luck Symbols. "Good Luck Horseshoe." Accessed on May 24, 2021. https://goodlucksymbols.com.

GRASPP. "Ghost Hunt aboard the LST 393." Youtube.com. October 23, 2019. Video, 11:24. Accessed on June 8, 2021. https://www.youtube.com.

Hackley-Hume Historic Site. "Fright Night at the Museum." Lakeshore Museum Center. 2021. Accessed September 13, 2021. https://lakeshoremuseum.org.

———. "Tour and Event Information." Lakeshore Museum Center. October 7, 2021. https://lakeshoremuseum.org.

Hackley Public Library. "History of the Library." https://www.hackleylibrary.org. Accessed January 13, 2022.

Hadley, Deanna, and Candi Hess. "Pastry Shop Investigation, Equipment and Investigative Methods." West Michigan Paranormal Team. Facebook group. www.facebook.com. Personal interview with author. March 18, 2021.

Haunted Hall. Facebook group. "The Northshore Hospital." May 7, 2012. Accessed August 11, 2021. www.facebook.com.

Hause, H.L. "Headlight Flashes along the Grand Trunk Railway System." *Muskegon Railroad Historical Periodical*. Chicago: Chicago Railroad Publishing, 1897.

Havis, Michael, and Harry Howard. "Shipwreck Hunters Solve Mystery of the Missing Griffon: Wreckage of 'Cursed' Vessel that Sunk in Lake Michigan on Its Maiden Voyage Is Identified Nearly 350 Years After It Vanished." *Daily Mail*, June 16, 2021. Accessed November 30, 2021. https://www.dailymail.co.uk.

Higgypop. "What Do Ghosts Actually Want & Why Do They Haunt Us?" September 12, 2017. Accessed on May 28, 2021. https://www.higgypop.com.

History Central. "LST 393." Accessed November 15, 2021. https://historycentral.com.

Hobson, Lois. "Discover Lakeside." Visit Muskegon. Accessed June 12, 2021. https://visitmuskegon.org.

Hoffius, Lisa, and Bill Moore. "Thomas Hume." Rootsweb. Accessed February 18, 2021. http://freepages.rootsweb.com.

Horn, Patrick, host. "The Century Club." *Muskegon History and Beyond with the Lakeshore Museum Center*. Podcast, 10:45. August 1, 2018. Accessed August 9, 2021. https://anchor.fm/patrick-horn.

———. "The Christmas Tree Ship." *Muskegon History and Beyond at Lakeshore Museum Center*. Podcast, 8:53. December 16, 2020. https://anchor.fm/patrick-horn.

———. "Hackley and Hume Historic Site." *Muskegon History and Beyond with Lakeshore Museum Center*. Podcast, 26:31. https://anchor.fm/patrick-horn.

———. "John Torrent—Lumberman, Inventor, Politician, and Real Estate Mogul." *Muskegon History and Beyond with Lakeshore Museum Center*. Podcast, 17:30. December, 5, 2018. https://anchor.fm/patrick-horn.

———. "The Name Game: Street Names of Muskegon County." Muskegon History and Beyond with Jackie Huss at Lakeshore Museum Center. Podcast, 13:12. March 18, 2018. https://anchor.fm/patrick-horn.

———. "A Station for All: Union Depot." *Muskegon History and Beyond with Lakeshore Museum Center*. Podcast, 8:24. January 2, 2019. https://anchor.fm/patrick-horn.

———. "The Streets of Muskegon County II." *Muskegon History and Beyond with Lakeshore Museum Center*. Podcast, 13:54. March 6, 2019. https://anchor.fm/patrick-horn.

Iddings, Bill. "Frauenthal Theater's 80th Anniversary Sparks Entertaining Memories." *Muskegon Chronicle*, September 12, 2010. Accessed August 5, 2021. https://www.mlive.com.

Jeltema, Ryan. "Lookback: Muskegon Lumber Baron's Mansion Was State-of-the-Art in Its Day." Mlive.com. April 30, 2012. Updated January 20, 2019. https://www.mlive.com.

"The John Torrent Story (1833–1915)" (flyer handout). Hackley Public Library, Local History and Genealogical Department. https://www.hackleylibrary.org.

Jones, Connie, and Bill Jones. "Frauenthal Theater, LST 393 Investigation, Paranormal Equipment and Investigative Methods." Gathering Research and Stories of Paranormal Phenomena (GRASSP). Facebook group. www.facebook.com. Personal interview with author. March 27, 2021.

Joslin, Jeff. "Muskegon Iron Works, Rogers Iron Manufacturing Company, Muskegon, Michigan, U.S.A." Vintage Machinery. December 14, 2015. http://vintagemachinery.org.

Keasling, Alyssa. "Spanish Renaissance." Design History. April 4, 2012. Accessed August 5, 2021. https://alyssakeasling.wordpress.com.

Kyes, Alice Prescott. *Romance of Muskegon*. Muskegon, MI: Muskegon Heritage Association, 1974.

Lakatos, Dava. "A Day in the Life of the U.S.S. 393." Military History of the Upper Great Lakes. October 27, 2019. https://ss.sites.mtu.edu/mhugl.

Lampkin, Virgina. "Christmas Tree Ghost Ship." Seeks Ghosts. November 17, 2014. Accessed May 24, 2021. https://seeksghosts.blogspot.com.

Lardinois, Anna. "The Legend of Lake Michigan's Captain Santa and His Christmas Tree Boat: Some Claim They Still See Herman Schuenemann's Ship Sailing on the Great Lake." *Milwaukee*, 2021. Accessed on May 26, 2021. https://www.milwaukeemag.com.

Larson, Agnes M. *The White Pine Industry in Minnesota: A History*. Minneapolis: University of Minnesota Press, 2007.

LeMieux, Dave. "Looking Back at Muskegon's Roseland Ballroom and Paul Schlossman's Legacy." *Muskegon Chronicle*, October 5, 2015. Accessed August 5, 2021. https://www.mlive.com.

Leonard, Taylor. "Five Reasons Why Renovations Trigger Paranormal Activity." The Ghost Dairies. July 2017. Accessed May 10, 2021. https://theghostdiaries.com.

Lewis, Adrian R. "Landing Ship, Tank." *Encyclopedia Britannica*. April 7, 2005. Accessed June 8, 2021. https://www.britannica.com.

Lijima, T.J. "The Great 19th Century Timber Heist Revisited." Foundation for Economic Education. April 9, 1990. Accessed February 12, 2021. https://fee.org.

Lipka, Michael. "18% of Americans Say They Have Seen a Ghost." Pew Research Center. October 30, 2015. Accessed April 21, 2021. https://www.pewresearch.org.

Little Giant Encyclopedia of Superstitions. "Rats." New York: Sterling Publishing, 1999.

Lolo, Andre. "13 Signs that You're An Empath." Highly Sensitive Refuge. January 18, 2019. https://highlysensitiverefuge.com.

LST 393 Veterans Museum. "LST 393 Landing Ship Tank." Veteran's Museum tour guide brochure. 2021. Mart Dock, Muskegon, Michigan.

Manitowoc Historical Society. "The Rouse-Simmons." Accessed May 26, 2021. www.manitowoccountyhistory.org.

Melina, Chris. "Explorer Believes He Has Found Great Lakes' Oldest Known Shpwreck." Wisconsin Public Radio. July 10, 2014. Accessed September 28, 2021. https://www.wpr.org.

Michigan Haunted Houses. "Nunica Cemetery: MI: Real Haunted Places." January 11, 2021. Accessed August 20, 2021. https://www.michiganhauntedhouses.com.

"Michigan Logging Railroad Era 1850–1963." Clark Historical Library at Central Michigan University. Digital collections. https://clarkedigitalcollections.cmich.edu.

Monroe, Alyssa. "What Is a Medium and How Are They Different than Psychics?" Psychics 4 Today. Accessed April 22, 2021. https://www.psychics4today.com.

———. "What Is Scrying and How Does It Work? Psychics 4 Today. Accessed May 6, 2021. https://www.psychics4today.com.

Morrison, Ryan, and Michael Havis. "Shipwreck Found in Lake Michigan May Be a Notorious 'Cursed' Ship." MSN. June 16, 2021. Accessed September 28, 2021. https://www.msn.com.

Muskegon Board of Trade. *Muskegon and Its Resources: Sketches of Muskegon County, Its Soil, Climate and Agricultural Producations—City of Muskegon, Its Material Growth and Resources, Manufacturing and Commercial Interests, Its Scenery, and Advantages as a Place of Residence and Business, Supplemented with Short Sketches of Leading Business Houses and Firms.* Ebook. Ann Arbor: University of Michigan, 1884.

Muskegon Chronicle. "The New Year Ushered in by Our Citizens in Good Shape." January 3, 1882.

Muskegon Community College. "Boogie Woogie Bugle Boy Sculpture Dedication at LST 393." November 10, 2018. Accessed January 7, 2022. https://www.muskegoncc.edu.

Muskegon County. "History of Muskegon." Accessed February 10, 2021. https://co.muskegon.m.us.

Muskegon Heritage Museum at the Lakeshore Museum Center. "Muskegon Brewing Company." Accessed September 13, 2021. https://lakeshoremuseum.org.

My Heritage. "Julia Hackley." January 13, 2022. Accessed January 13, 2022. https://www.myheritage.com.

National Institutes of Health Library of Medicine. History of Medicine. "Visual Culture and Public Health Posters, Tuberculosis." September 23, 2003. Accessed August 13, 2021.

Newkirk, Greg. "The Estes Method: How the Ground-Breaking SB7 Spirit Box Experiment Is Changing Paranormal Investigation." Paranormal Searchers, January 29, 2019. https://parasearcher.blogspot.com.

Nickell, Joe. *The Science of Ghosts: Searching for Spirits of the Dead*. Amherst, NY: Prometheus Books, 2012.

Noir, Shetan. "*The Rouse-Simmons. Christmas Tree Ship*." Personal zoom interview. M4A audio file recording, 18.8 MB, 20:31. Interviewed by Marie Cisneros, April 22, 2021.

Ohio History Central. "Rene R. De La Salle." November 29, 2021. Accessed November 30, 2021. https://ohiohistorycentral.org.

Osteopathic Foundation of West Michigan. "A History of Osteopathic Medicine in West Michigan." https://osteopathicfoundation.org.

The Other Side TV. "How to Use Dowsing Rods in An Investigation." Season 6. 2021. Accessed on May 6, 2021. https://theothersidetv.ca.

Painter, Sally. "The Legends and Disappearances at the Michigan Triangle." Top Secret Writers. 2015. https://www.topsecretwriters.com.

Pisacreta, Sharon. "Lost to the Lake: The Griffon. Lake Michigan's First Ghost Ship." Lake Effect Living. 2010. Accessed September 28, 2021. http://lakeeffectliving.com.

Robinson, John. "Haunted Michigan: The Cemetery Ghost Who Holds Your Hand." WFMK 99.1. October 17, 2017. Accessed August 20, 2021. https://99wfmk.com.

———. "Haunted Michigan: The Grounds of Northshore Hospital, Muskegon." WFMK 99.1. August 24, 2020. Accessed August 11, 2021. https://99wfmk.com.

Schmidt, Daniel, and Brandon Hoezee. "Torrent House Investigation, Paranormal Equipment and Investigative Methods." Kent County Paranormal. Personal interview with Marie Cisneros. March 16, 2021.

SFWeekly. "What Is a Clairvoyant? Your Questions about Clairvoyants and Clairvoyant Psychic Abilities Answered." November 6, 2020. https://www.sfweekly.com.

Sonnenberg, Mike. "The Historic Hume House." Lost in Michigan, December 14, 2018. https://lostinmichigan.net.

Taylor, Courtney. "The Probability of Being Dealt a Royal Flush in Poker." ThoughtCo. July 16, 2019. Accessed August 10, 2021. https://www.thoughtco.com.

Third Eye Paranormal Society. "Professional Ghost-Hunting Equipment—A Comprehensive List." Accessed on April 22, 2021. https://www.thirdeyeparanormalsociety.com.

13 on Your Side. "Creepy Flashlight Tours Offered after Dark at Hackley and Hume Homes." Youtube. October 13, 2020. Video, 2:01. Accessed September 3, 2021. https://www.youtube.com.
———. "Haunted Tours of Historic Homes in Muskegon." YouTube. October 18, 2019. Video, 5:08. https://www.youtube.com.
Vasquez, Dr. Alejandra. "What Is Ghost Sickness, and How Does it Work?" Cake. May 5, 2020. https://www.joincake.com.
Wagner, Steven. "What to Do With Your Premonitions: How to Handle Your Visions of Future Events, Great or Small." LiveAbout.com. Updated February 9, 2019. https://www.liveabout.com.
Wantz, E. Terry. "History of Newaygo County Railroads." Migenweb. Accessed on February 18, 2021. http://www.migenweb.org.
Weiser-Alexander, Kathy. "Ottawa Indian Tribe." Legends of America. Accessed February 16, 2021. https://www.legendsofamerica.com.
Wikipedia. "Charles Hackley." Updated January 15, 2022. https://en.wikipedia.org.
———. "Chicago and Lake Michigan Railroad." Updated November 13, 2019. Accessed February 23, 2020. https://en.wikipedia.org.
———. "Lake Michigan." May 11, 2021. Accessed on June 2, 2021. https://en.wikipedia.org.
———. "Lath and Plaster." Accessed on May 11, 2021. https://en.wikipedia.org.
———. "Michigan." Accessed March 1, 2021. https://en.wikipedia.org.
———. "Michigan Lakeshore Railroad." Updated August 26, 2020. Accessed February 23, 2020. https://en.wikipedia.org.
———. "Muskegon, Michigan." Accessed May 12, 2021. https://en.wikipedia.org.
———. "Nunica, Michigan." Accessed August 20, 2021. https://en.wikipedia.org.
———. "Rene de Brehant de Galinee." Accessed December 1, 2021. https://en.wikipedia.org.
———. "Rouse-Simmons." Accessed May 25, 2021. https://en.wikipedia.org.
———. "Union Depot, Muskegon, Michigan." Updated June 27, 2021. Accessed February 24, 2020. https://en.wikipedia.org.
Willi, Dawn. *Paranormal? I Believe…Maybe?* (blog), August 23, 2016. Accessed on July 15, 2021. https://paranormalbelievemaybe.blogspot.com.

World History. "The Rouse-Simmons, the Story of the Christmas Tree Ship." May 27, 2017. https://worldhistory.us.

Yates, Charles H. "Bluffton Has Seen Many Changes Since Its Village Days in 1880s." *Muskegon Chronicle*, January 18, 1958.

ABOUT THE AUTHOR

Marie Cisneros became a transplanted Michigander around the age of five, when she and her family moved to Muskegon, Michigan. Before that, Marie lived in the outskirts of Laredo, Texas, in a barrio known as "Ghost Town." Her love of exploration, research, history and the unknown was instilled early on with the family's frequent outings into the foothills and back brushes, where history was alive in the land. They would often find ancient Clovis arrowheads or interesting rocks, once even finding bones—human bones.

Her love of research really came into focus at the age of thirteen on the day she picked up her first books on ghosts, witches and UFOs. With this, her foray into world of the mysterious, unknown, hidden and spiritual began in earnest.

Marie is an investigative journalist, professional astrologer, UFOlogist, numerologist and ULC minister. She has an AAS and a BS in the medical sciences and had worked in the medical field for over twenty-five years. Her personal interests include acrylic painting, mixed-media art, jewelry design and crafting. She is also chief researcher for her own company, Cygnus Research.

She was a UFO field investigator for over ten years with the Mutual UFO Network (MUFON), investigating over one hundred cases in Michigan,

Kansas, Oregon and Montana, as well as a columnist for the *MUFON Journal*. She was also an investigative journalist, writer and media host for a local paranormal show. She has been featured on numerous UFOlogy and paranormal podcasts, radio and cable television broadcasts. She was a contributor to a well-known UFOlogy website, with her article being picked up worldwide and reprinted on hundreds of other UFOlogy websites.

Her love of exploring the unknown has never wavered and never will, as it is the search for all things mysterious, hidden and bizarre or that "go bump in the night" that makes this girl from Ghost Town come alive.